Dwight Longenecker

CATHOLICISM
Pure & Simple

CATHOLICISM

Pure and Simple

Dwight Longenecker

𝒮.

STAUFFER
BOOKS

STAUFFER
BOOKS

STAUFFER BOOKS
Terra Lane, Greenville, SC

✺

COVER DESIGN & BOOK LAYOUT
Christopher J. Pelicano

PRINTED AND BOUND IN THE U.S.A
CreateSpace

COVER ARTWORK
Rembrandt van Rijn
Head of Christ

✺

ISBN 978-0-615673-89-9

What people are saying about
Catholicism: Pure and Simple ...

"Father Dwight Longenecker does for Catholicism what C. S. Lewis did for "mere Christianity". Those looking for the way home by taking the path to Rome will find this book an excellent and reliable guide for the journey."

—Joseph Pearce, author of *C.S.Lewis and the Catholic Church*

"Convert Father Dwight makes a powerfully "pure and simple" presentation of the Catholic faith. From fundamentalist Protestant to Anglican to Catholic; from America to England and back again; he asked difficult questions, and in this fine text, he successfully presents the answers that helped him make his journey home."

—Marcus Grodi, host EWTN's *Journey's Home*, author of *How Firm a Foundation* and *Pillar and Bulwark*

" In *Catholicism Pure and Simple*, Fr Dwight Longenecker walks readers from the existence of God, through the doors of the Church, and eventually all the way to heaven covering the basic teachings with constant warmth and wit… *Catholicism Pure and Simple* is perfect for skeptics, doubters, and spiritual fledglings. It may be pure and simple, but it's also enjoyable and smart from beginning to end."

—Brandon Vogt, blogger and author of *The Church and the New Media*

"*Catholicism Pure and Simple* is just what we need for seekers with questions and Catholics with doubts.. I loved Fr. Longenecker's incisive, witty style, and the way he gets into the heads of readers and understands what they need in order to discover the eternal treasures of the Catholic Church."

—Ronda Chervin Ph.D., Professor of Philosophy, Holy Apostles College and Seminary and Catholic author

"The book title says it all. Father Longenecker guides us through salvation history and the role of the Catholic Church, with a simple style we can all understand... I found myself nodding "yes" in joyful agreement through each chapter."

—Tom Peterson, President and Founder, Catholics Come Home, Inc.

"Fr. Dwight Longenecker likes to give us Jesus straight up and with a generous dollop of joy. He takes the newbie through the life of the Faith in a way that whets your appetite, makes you curious and cracks you up."

—Mark P. Shea, blogger, journalist and author of *The Heart of Catholic Prayer*

"*Catholicism Pure and Simple* is meat and potatoes for those malnourished by the fast food buffet of secular materialism and the new paganism... I am responsible for helping adults understand and live the faith, and this is the book I have been looking for. It explains the Catholic faith in refreshingly plain language - while opening the reader to its depth and beauty and inviting them to go deeper....Buy a box full and give them away!"

—Deacon Keith Fournier, Editor in Chief of Catholic Online

" Fr. Longenecker has written another gem. Written with clarity and straight talk and directly from Fr. Longenecker's priestly heart; the title says it all: *Catholicism Pure and Simple*... This is an excellent book for anyone who wants to become Catholic or for any Catholic who wants to learn more about the Faith... use this book as a textbook for confirmation and RCIA. Evangelize by getting more copies to spread around.

—Fr. James Farfaglia, author of *Get Serious!-A Survival Guide for Serious Catholics*

"DaVinci observed, "Simplicity, is the ultimate sophistication"—and Father Longenecker's prose is both svelte and sophisticated. In *Catholicism Pure and Simple*, he uses wit and an abundance of grace to bring the most complex theological propositions within reach of all."

—Kathy Schiffer, blogger, Seasons of Grace

"Fr. Longenecker's *Catholicism Pure and Simple* successfully communicates the basic truths of Catholicism in a refreshingly straightforward and direct manner. For anyone interested in exploring the Catholic faith, this is a great place to start."

—Hector Molina, Catholic Speaker and Evangelist

"Fr. Longenecker provides an invaluable service for inquirers by explaining the Catholic faith in a personable, accessible, yet concise fashion, and clearing away many common misconceptions. Highly recommended!"

—Dave Armstrong, author of 30 Catholic apologetics books, including *100 Biblical Arguments Against Sola Scriptura* and *The Quotable Newman*

" Fr. Longenecker does something in *Catholicism Pure and Simple* that is difficult to do: he presents the truths of the Catholic faith in a clear, easy to understand manner and yet loses nothing of its depth and beauty. Whether a person is new to Christianity or has been raised Catholic this book is bound to inform and inspire."

—Chris Stewart, President of Casting Nets Ministries

CONTENTS

CONTENTS

THE GREAT BATTLE

WELCOME HOME

CATHOLICISM
Pure & Simple

One of the problems with our modern world is that there is too much religion out there. The market is flooded, not only with thousands of different forms of Christianity, but a whole shopping mall of other religions, self help programs, new age techniques and strange philosophies. The internet is crowded with ideas, ideologies and religions of all kinds. Everybody is looking for the answer to life's riddles, but there are too many different answers being offered.

Furthermore, the traditional forms of Christianity, like Catholicism, are weighed down with liturgies that are difficult to understand, complex theological theories, rules and regulations that seem complicated, and a hierarchy and bureaucracy which seems top heavy, cumbersome and sometimes corrupt. Added to these problems, Catholicism either comes across as ancient, irrelevant and out of touch—or even worse—as trying hard to be up to date, trendy and "with it".

There's more: for the last five hundred years, in many parts of our culture, there has been a lingering anti-Catholic bias. Generations of non-Catholics have been brought up with an underlying assumption that Catholicism is simply wrong. They have been taught that the Catholic faith is a religion of superstitious foreigners who worship statues; that the Popes are all rich, corrupt and power hungry despots; that Catholic priests are scheming, greedy men and that the whole Catholic church is, wealthy, powerful and far from the simple religion of the carpenter Jesus Christ.

This centuries-old bias against Catholicism has been made worse with recent financial and sexual scandals which the media keeps before the eyes of the public relentlessly. All these problems contribute to a new form of anti-Catholicism which is ever more popular in society. It could be called "atheism lite". This new breed of atheists have picked up their beliefs from the vast melting pot of popular culture. A newspaper article here, a website there, here a book by a new atheist, there a lecture by a college professor: all of it leads to an ill formed and half thought out, but passionately held "atheism" which is usually no more than a thinly disguised anti-Catholicism.

Catholicism Pure & Simple

As a result, there is a desperate need for *Catholicism Pure and Simple*. This book presents the basics of the Catholic faith in simple, straightforward language. You will not find here complex philosophical arguments, insider churchy talk or complicated theological language. I have avoided hi-falutin' references and obscure quotations. There aren't any academic notes or quotes in Greek, Latin and Aramaic. This is meat and potatoes religion.

This book does not answer all the questions or make all the arguments. It simply starts by explaining why we believe God exists, and then goes on, step by step to explain who Jesus Christ is, what his life and death mean and how the Catholic Church came about. It explains what it means to be a Catholic and how one lives the Catholic faith.

This book does not hold the complete teachings of the Catholic faith. You'll find that in the *Catechism of the Catholic Church*. This book is a starting point, not a final destination. If you read this book and want to know more about the Catholic faith, the next step, if you have not done so already, is to join an RCIA course at your local Catholic Church. "RCIA" stands for "Rite of Christian Initiation for Adults." RCIA courses usually begin in the Autumn and last for about eight months. Those who have completed an RCIA course are usually received into the Catholic Church at Easter after they have done the course.

This book is an excellent text book for someone who is in RCIA or confirmation class. It also provides an excellent back-up and refresher course for Catholics to know their faith better.

I hope and pray that *Catholicism Pure & Simple* will help you get past any difficulties you have in under-standing the Catholic faith and see Catholicism in its simplicity and purity. At its heart, the Catholic faith is an encounter with Jesus Christ—an encounter that can change your life for the better, and set you on the path not only to a more complete and joyful life, but also to a final peace and joy that is beyond all human imagining.

SECTION ONE

IS ANYBODY THERE?

Chapter One

The Religious Instinct

Have you ever stopped to consider how strange it is that human beings are religious?

We're told that humans are the most highly evolved form of animal life. We are rational beings. We can think and speak and write and read and reason and argue. We can do experiments and think logically and work out problems with our vast intellect. It is said that we are the most amazingly intelligent and rational animals the world has ever seen.

But at the same time the vast majority of humans are religious. On the one hand we are rational and reasonable. On the other hand we believe in a spiritual world inhabited by invisible beings. We say that each human has an invisible dimension called an eternal soul. We read books we believe are inspired by angels or by God. We build temples, mosques and churches, discuss theology, light candles, pray and believe in heaven and hell and miracles. We're rational, but we have this

1

religious instinct, and it's curious. It's strange. We're not just apes. We're apes longing to be angels.

I don't mean that everyone goes to church every Sunday, or that all people everywhere believe in God and practice a religion faithfully. I just mean that no matter where or when they have lived, the vast majority of human beings have acted on a gut-level instinct that there is more to life than meets the eye, and that someone else is "out there."

Some would argue that this strange religious instinct is a leftover from our more primitive stages of development, and that to be purely rational is to be more highly developed. But what if it were the other way around, and our religious instinct and spiritual capacity is the higher form of development? Maybe dealing rationally with the physical world is the more primitive part of us, while the capacity to interact abstractly with an unseen realm is the highest point of our human development.

Perhaps the religious instinct unlocks the true mystery and glory of humanity. Maybe the ability to pray and worship is mankind's highest accomplishment. If so, where did this religious instinct come from? It seems to be a universal human capability. Human beings respond to their world in a religious way instinctively. In times of danger they cry out for protection. It times of need they ask for help, and in times of peace and plenty they pause to give thanks. When faced with the awesome force of nature or the miracle of a new-born child, they instinctively look beyond themselves to a greater power. This shared religious instinct is one of the things that sets humans apart from the animals. A wolf might howl at the moon, but he doesn't worship the moon goddess. A dog might roll over and play dead, but he does not kneel and pray for the dead. A gorilla may play, but he does not pray.

Human beings, on the other hand, do this religious thing. In every society and culture from the most primitive to the most sophisticated, people have told stories about gods, built temples, established rituals, and honored men and women they thought were above the others because they were heroically holy.

It's easy to think that religion is the last vestige of a primitive society, but in the modern world religion is as popular as ever. The signs of this religious instinct are everywhere. We may have satellites and cell phones, jets and laptops and amazing engineering and marvelous communications, but still we gather to worship God and turn our hearts toward heaven.

Travel across the world and you find that all the greatest monuments and buildings have religious purpose. Everywhere you come across temples and shrines of every shape and kind, from Stonehenge to St. Peter's Basilica, from a simple Baptist church to the temples of Angkor Wat, from the ruins of a makeshift shrine in a cell at Auschwitz to the Parthenon, Chartres Cathedral, or a Buddhist pagoda. Look further and you will see a range of institutions, charities, hospitals, schools and colleges all started, maintained and funded because of the religious instinct.

In a multitude of fascinating, bewildering, and strange ways human beings have been motivated by their religious instinct. The religious instinct has driven both individuals and empires, and has produced the greatest literature, art, architecture, music, education, health care and charitable work the world has ever seen. Furthermore, in all its different forms, religion is a stronger force in the world than it has ever been. Rather than dying out in the modern age, religion is increasing in fervor and strength across the globe.

This religious instinct isn't just a quirk of one group of people—it's virtually universal. Religion is so common to humanity that we can say it is an integral part of our nature; being religious is as natural to human beings as swimming is to fish.

Why do we have this religious instinct? Where does it come from? Whether we are religious or not, we must see this strange phenomenon and ask ourselves why it is that virtually all human beings everywhere have believed in some sort of God.

If you've ever stopped to ask this question you may already have come up with what you think is a good answer. This book is designed to help you stop and think again and really examine all the possibilities.

Something New and Strange

The religious instinct can be found everywhere, and in all times down through human history, but in recent years something new and strange has developed: some people have come to disbelieve in the existence of God. Widespread atheism is unique in human history, but because we are so used to it today, we don't realize how strange it is.

In our society, for all sorts of reasons, ordinary people have been taught—by their parents, their schools, their governments—not to believe the existence of God. Therefore, before we can discuss religion, we need to stop and ask why we believe God exists in the first place. It's a good thing to take time for this thought process whether you already believe in God or not.

For the believer, explaining the existence of God is a tricky exercise. It is a bit like trying to explain the existence of love to someone who has never been in love.

To explain the existence of love you would have to use intellectual language for something that is much bigger than just clever ideas and arguments. The words you used would sound awkward and inadequate. Furthermore, even if you were to convince the person who doesn't believe in love that such a thing as love exists, he still wouldn't understand what it's like to be in love. Your effort wouldn't really succeed. You would end up frustrated and think the whole exercise wasn't worth the bother.

Nevertheless, we still have to try to give good reasons for the existence of God. Such explanations are like the instruction you have to take before an exciting sport like water skiing or skydiving.

You're always tempted to skip the training and get on with the real thing, but without the training you might make critical mistakes. The arguments for the existence of God require some brain work, but this basic training lays the necessary foundations, and we skip it at our peril.

Atheists or Animals?

If a human being lives only for the basic physical needs of food, shelter, safety and sex then he is no better than an animal. It might seem like some people live that way, but even the most brutal humans live for something more.

Atheists don't believe God exists. But I don't believe *atheists* exist.

I don't believe atheists exist because they are not animals. They are not animals because they believe in something greater than themselves. Even the most atheistic person lives for something, and unless he is a totally depraved and wicked person, he lives for something he believes is good.

Maybe he is passionate about truth, and spends his life exposing fakes and searching for truth. Although he denies that there is a God, perhaps the atheist spends his whole life pursuing justice and peace. He might spend his life doing good and helping people. If he does, he is living for something greater than himself.

Perhaps the atheist lives for love. Even if the atheist flits from one boyfriend or girlfriend to another, deep down he or she is looking for a love that will last forever.

Dwight Longenecker

Maybe the atheist lives only for what he thinks is "the good life"—in other words, for his own personal pleasure; but even that is good, simply because it gives him pleasure, which is good. His pursuit of pleasure also shows that he believes there is such a thing as happiness. It's true that his pursuit of pleasure may lead him to behave selfishly, and he will end up being unsatisfied, but even so, he is still living his life in the pursuit of something he believes is good.

If most "atheists" live their lives seeking something good, then they believe in something good, and if they believe in something good—something so good that they are willing to work hard to get it—then they believe some kind of Goodness or Happiness exists which is outside themselves and greater than themselves.

There must be an ultimate Good outside themselves otherwise why is this Happiness so difficult to discover? If Happiness were totally within ourselves then physical pleasure would satisfy us, but we know it doesn't. This Goodness or Happiness they seek is elusive. It's hard to obtain and retain. It is easily lost. Therefore it must be something greater than themselves and their own basic physical instincts.

This ultimate Happiness they are pursuing is a Good they believe in. Even if they deny it, they are pursuing not just a Good, but a god. Compared to the God of religious people, the atheist's god is a very little god, and a god of their own making, but it is still a kind of 'god' because it is a source of Ultimate goodness and reality greater than themselves for which they strive and live.

7

CATHOLICISM / *Pure and Simple*

The Cave Man and the Stars

If we were just animals we would be satisfied with food, sex, shelter and comfort; but we're not. We long for something else. This desire to live for something good that is greater than ourselves is part of the universal human religious instinct. Why should this desire for some great good be there at all? How did we develop this idea that there is something good worth living for, or some great being out there that we ought to worship and obey?

Some people believe it is simply a matter of how we evolved. The cave man, they suggest, looked up at the sun, moon, and stars and was filled with wonder and fear at their greatness. He heard the thunder, saw the lightning and imagined that some great being like him lived in the clouds. He imagined that this being was sometimes angry and sometimes pleased, because sometimes he blessed the man with rain and sunshine and other times punished him with drought and disaster.

The cave man concluded that this big chief on the other side of the clouds needed to be satisfied and kept happy, and all the rest of religion with its complicated doctrines, rules, and rituals started to evolve.

Do you notice how this argument makes certain assumptions about cave men? It treats the cave man as a noble savage. Because he feels a sense of wonder at the natural world he is portrayed as an ignorant, but touchingly sensitive brute; but have you seen the trick? Because he is a cave man we assume that he must be inferior to us; therefore his conclusion that there is a big person beyond the clouds who caused the thunder must also be primitive, and wrong.

Although cave men may not have been as educated as we are or have such whiz-bang technology, were they really so much stupider? Are we sure cave men wore animal skins, grunted, and dragged their women around by their hair? We don't have evidence for that. Instead, when their graves are opened we find beautiful works of art and craftsmanship, and when we go into the cave itself we find mysterious and beautiful wall paintings. The evidence we have tells us that whoever painted those graceful bison and deer were not primitive brutes, but sensitive artists.

If those cave artists observed the natural world with such sensitivity, they must also have gazed at the stars with awesome wonder, and perhaps they were frightened by the thunder. If this is so, were they really so very different from us? Which of us hasn't tried to paint a landscape, or sketch our beloved? Which of us has not been filled with wonder on a starlit night or frightened by a hurricane, flood or tornado?

If the cave man felt awe and wonder in the face of nature's power, is that really a sign of stupidity? Isn't it rather a sign of their heartfelt humanity? Is the cave man's feeling of awe and wonder a sign of his being thickheaded, or is our lack of awe and wonder a sign of our being hard hearted?

The Caveman's Conclusion

The caveman is being quite sensible, in his own way, to observe nature and see the signs of an unseen intelligence. Like most easy theories, this theory of where our religious instinct comes from is both right and wrong. It is right because it tells us that even primitive people can see the power of nature and conclude that there is a mind behind it all.

However, the theory is wrong in what it assumes. It assumes that because modern humans understand the physics of thunder, and have telescopes to study the stars, that they no longer have a need for God. Saying there is no God simply because you understand how nature works, is like saying Henry Ford never existed because you have done a course on car mechanics.

The other thing the cave man got right was his idea that whoever was "out there" was stronger than he was. Because the Great Spirit in the Sky was stronger, it would have been logical for the cave man to be afraid of him, and if he was frightened he might also, quite sensibly draw the conclusion that the Sky God was also angry, and needed to be kept happy.

As a basic starting point for religion, it sounds like common sense doesn't it? If the cave man then started to think further about his discovery, and came to the idea that this Being was probably not all bad and fearsome, that too makes sense. Humans are always exploring their discoveries and learning more about them.

The question of how the human religious instinct developed is fascinating; but for now let's assume that the cave man was right.

In the forces of nature, he sensed a larger force. He instinctively sensed that the forces of nature had to have some ultimate, final cause. The cave man may not have thought it all through logically, but like a child, he sensed this force, and responded with fascination and curiosity. He sensed that someone else was "out there" and he wanted to know more.

This curiosity lies at the root of our own religious instinct too. No matter who we are, we sense that there is more to life than meets the eye. Like the cave man, we see the beauty of the natural world; we marvel at the stars and tremble at the rolling thunder, but we also sense that we are part of this marvelous, mysterious world, and that the force behind it is also behind our own lives.

This unknown force exerts a powerful magnetic influence on us. We want to learn more about this mysterious presence, and that is what the religious quest is all about.

Chapter Two
Slam on the Brakes!

You may have come along with this discussion so
far with no problem. You can see how the religious instinct started in the human race, and maybe you don't
have any arguments.

If so, you're making it too easy. If you don't already,
you should have some demanding questions.

When I said that the religious instinct is common to
all human beings maybe you wanted to ask why there
are so many different religions. It's a good question.
How the different religions relate to each other will
become clear as the book develops.

When I said that religion has been the source for
some of the greatest achievements of the human
race you may have wanted to reply, "But religion is
also the source for the worst things in history! What
about terrorism, witch hunts, the Spanish Inquisi-
tion, and all the religious wars around the world?
What about the abuse of children, the greed and

guilt and power grabs all in the name of religion!"

It's true that terrible things have happened because of misplaced religious zeal (though probably not as terrible or as many as people think). Some religious people have abused religion for their own ends, but we can't dismiss all religion because of the bad things that have happened, any more than we can dismiss patriotism and love of country because there are tyrants and generals who have waged war for the sake of their country. Not everyone who loves their country is mad and bad, and even the bad ones don't invalidate the proper love of country.

Likewise, if virtually the entire human race has a religious instinct; there must be something to it even if some religious people are evil or crazy.

If you're thinking this through at all you should also be asking questions not just about evil religious people, but the whole existence of Evil. You know how the question goes, "If there is an all-loving, all-powerful God, why does he allow such terrible suffering in the world?" This is the best question anybody can ask about the problem of God.

Everyone is right to ask how we can possibly believe in a God who allows the horrors of concentration camps, terrorism, war, starvation, and natural disasters. I hope you don't mind if I put that question to the side for now. It's not that the question can't be answered. Rather, the question is so important that I have to devote quite a bit of space to it in the next chapter.

The other reason I'd like to put that particular question to the side is because there are some other problems that need to be considered just to make sure the foundation for an answer is laid properly.

The question about suffering and an all loving God is jumping the gun a bit, because we've only begun to consider the probability that some sort of God is out there. We haven't decided what that God is like. In other words, we haven't yet got to the point where God is all-powerful and all-loving. We're still discussing whether he exists at all.

For now we're thinking about the origins of the religious instinct, and one of the answers is that people came up with the idea of God and religion because they faced the stark reality of death and needed a way out. They needed some way to believe that they wouldn't die, but live forever.

The Security Blanket God

God then becomes a kind of security blanket. The theory goes like this: "Evolution has ingrained in us the desire to survive. However, we know death is around the corner, so the natural instinct is to deny death and hope that somehow we might go on living. Therefore immature and weak people cling to the hope that there is a great and good Sugar Daddy in the sky who will keep them alive and eternally happy."

On the surface, this sounds plausible. It's easy to draw that conclusion because Christianity *does* worship a God who offers eternal life. However, that's not the way religion started. Most of the gods of primitive people were fearsome beings who didn't promise eternal life. In fact, they didn't promise anything to anybody. Instead of offering life they demanded death.

A large part of religious practice for many primitive religions was the offering of human sacrifices to keep the terrifying gods happy. There was no idea of eternal life for the individual believer. If you followed a primitive religion the only thing you could hope for was that if your god was satisfied he would make sure your harvest was good, your tribe was healthy and that you were protected from the enemy tribe.

The idea of individuals enjoying life after death is a recent development in the history of religion. Cultural historians tell us that that people worshipped gods and goddesses before they had the idea of an afterlife for themselves. Therefore, the idea that the religious instinct is the product of our desire to live forever can't be true.

Religion is Just Wishful Thinking!

"Nevertheless," you might say, "the whole religious enterprise is just a form of wishful thinking. Because this life is hard, people imagine that a good God in heaven will make them happy in the next life."

It is true that some people worship a God who is like a big vending machine. They put prayer and worship in, and they expect God to deliver whatever they want.

This is a superstitious and immature form of religion. *Real* religion doesn't just dish out shallow happiness. Rather than fulfilling our wishes, real religion challenges our wishes.

This is true of all religions. They make the most strenuous demands on people. All the great religions enforce strict moral codes. Jesus Christ says, "You cannot be my disciple unless you take up your cross and follow me." In other words, authentic religion doesn't offer an easy life. Just the reverse—it offers a life that is rigorous and demanding.

Is God just a big, happy grandfather in the sky who religious people vainly hope will make them happy one day?

It is true that we hope for final happiness. It is also true that we believe God loves us. But God's love is not sweet and fluffy like cotton candy. Instead, it is solid, severe, and awesome. Remember, those who believe in a God who rewards them, also believe that the reward will be just.

In other words God is their judge. If God is their judge, then he holds them accountable for every decision and action of their lives. This is not exactly a cozy idea. If I were thinking wishfully, this is not the kind of God I would have wished for.

Something Has to Keep Society Together

Other people argue that religion did not come about because of wishful thinking, but because society needed it.

"As people began to live in communities," they explain, "they needed certain taboos like, "you must not sleep with your brother's wife" or "you must not kill pregnant cows." Before long they saw that religion could help enforce these necessary taboos.

The Great Being in the sky was invoked as an ultimate source of punishment. If you broke the taboos you not only endangered the tribe, but God might punish you. For people with this opinion, religion is simply part of a necessary social structure. Over time this religion became complex and ornate, and full of doctrines, rituals and regulations.

It is true that religion helps to support our families and our communities. But can that be the only source of our religious instinct? I don't think so, for two reasons. First, religion was there before the social taboos were. The first religious instinct had nothing to do with rules, and the first religions were simply rituals to keep the unpredictable gods happy. Because religion came before rules, the rules cannot be the root source for religion.

Second, while religion supports society, it also criticizes it. The priest, pastor, or prophet may work with the ruling power, but history shows that in virtually every society, religious leaders have also felt obliged to contradict the worldly rulers and point out where society is going wrong. The martyrs of every religion have been willing to die because of their opposition to the rules of the society in which they lived.

＊

Because religion came before rules, and because religion often finds itself at odds with society, we have to conclude that religion must be both older and bigger than society.

What You See is What you Get?

There are some very practically minded people who object to God and religion because they say there is no evidence. We have to ask therefore what they will admit as evidence for God's existence. If they want scientifically verifiable evidence then they will be disappointed.

Asking for scientific proof of God's existence is a nonsense question. To do so is like the dull boy who took apart a clock to find time.

Asking for physical proof for God's existence is like asking for proof of the existence of energy. Energy is everywhere. We assume its existence because we see its effects. We can understand the sources of energy and the forms it takes. We can devise theories about how energy changes and how energy behaves, but if I wanted to obstinately doubt the existence of energy how could anyone prove its existence?

If you wanted to talk to me about atoms and electrons, neutrons and protons I could say you were talking about invisible things that are all in your imagination. If you explained that these atoms were the foundation for all things and that energy was in and through all things and made them move I could say you were talking a fairy tale language. You might explain that, while you can't see atoms there is so much indirect evidence that we assume their existence. You could explain all about the complexities of energy and I might say it was all falderol—that things just are. That's all. There's no such thing as your fairy tale "energy" and your atoms and electrons and so forth are all an extravagant fiction.

But I would be wrong. There are some things that we take on observation, universal human experience, common sense and the experience and knowledge of those who know more than we do.

Nevertheless, some atheists reply that the whole idea of God is too complex.

"Look," they say, "all this complicated theological talk and religious fol-di-rol is just hogwash. The world simply is. What you see is what you get. There is no God up there. There is no ultimate meaning and no plan. What you think is a marvelous pattern in the world has been projected there by your own mind. Human beings can't face the fact that the universe is empty so they make up a big story about a Creator who plans everything. But there is no such thing. There is no meaning. The universe just is. That's it. End of story."

This theory is stunning in its simplicity. "The whole cosmos simply is. That's it. No need for meaning and purpose."

However, we cannot deny the laws of nature. The natural world obeys certain laws which scientists can explain. The physical world operates like a complex and intricate inter-related machine. The physical world is not simple.

Indeed, the closer we look at the natural world, the more complex it becomes. It turns out that the intricate study of molecular biology is as complex and mysterious as the infinite study of astrophysics.

Reality is more vast, flexible and complicated than we had first thought. Just as the scientist observes the world, seeks to discover how it works, and draws certain conclusions based on the evidence, so the religious person explores and observes a different aspect of reality and proposes theories and explanations about it. Man does not just search for a mechanical understanding of reality. He also searches for meaning. If there were no meaning, why this relentless search to find it?

The atheist would say that the person searching for meaning is chasing a pot of gold at the end of the rainbow. It's simple: there is no meaning or purpose.

I Speak Therefore I Am

If the universe has no meaning or purpose, then it must be random and meaningless.

But if everything is random, how would it be possible for someone to say so, since to think and speak you have to use language—which has order, structure and grammar?

Look at it this way: Language has meaning. The whole process of thinking and speaking is logical. It is patterned, planned, and complex. If there is no plan or pattern in the universe how could such a thing as human thought and language even come about?

Could we think logically in a universe that is random? If everything were random all we could do would be to grunt at each other and wave our arms like madmen. Therefore, as soon as you say, "The universe has no meaning or pattern." You have proved yourself wrong because you have thought and said something with meaning, pattern and purpose.

This train of thought is more like a train wreck. Because, when you think about it, everything in the world may pile up in a crash behind it.

What I mean is: if there is no meaning or pattern to the universe—if all meaning is just in our mind, then the whole world including ourselves, may also be no more than a random figment of our imagination. Is it really common sense to say that everything is just a dream inside our heads—that everything is no more than a series of chemical reactions going fizz-pop in our brains?

I don't think so. Nevertheless, it's a good question because it makes us come up with the conclusion that either everything is random and meaningless or it is not.

The Master Builder

There are only two choices: the whole universe is random and meaningless, or it is reasonable and meaningful. If it is random and meaningless, then it is difficult to account for the complex, structured world we inhabit, and the complex, structured minds with which we think and the complex, structured and meaningful language we use.

We must conclude that this complex, structured and intricate universe happened by random, or that it did not happen by random. If it did not happen randomly, then it happened as the result of some purpose or intention, and one cannot have purpose or intention without a purposeful mind and intentional will.

This is why philosophers and cavemen have concluded that behind the intelligent design of nature there is an intelligent designer.

The question about the ultimate origin of all things is the basic religious question. It is at the heart of the awe and wonder we feel when faced with nature, and it is the question which has led countless inquiring souls to meet God.

The beauty and complexity of the world, and the need for some force to be behind all movement in the world doesn't give us watertight proof for the existence of God, but on the basis of our common sense and the universal experience of the human race, it is not unreasonable to conclude that there is a God. We can give the proposal the benefit of the doubt. We are on solid ground.

However, accepting an intelligent designer for the universe is not the same thing as accepting the Christian God. The first step on this journey is to accept the possibility that there may be a God—that such a thing is, at least, possible and reasonable. This first step acknowledges that the religious instinct in human beings connects us to some intelligent force that is beyond all our thoughts, wishes, dreams and needs.

If we have got that far, and are really convinced, then the next thing we need to ask is whether that Some*thing* is a Someone. If this force of creation and power exists, is it simply a blind intelligence like a vast computer? It is just a vague energy source, or does it have a personality?

Chapter Three
Can the Force Be With You?

In *Star Wars*, Obi-Wan Kenobi explains to Luke Sky-walker that "the Force" is the power behind the created universe, and that you can either fight for the good side of the force, or be seduced by the dark side. The *Star Wars* films were a roaring success not only because of the great storytelling and special effects, but also be-cause they weave into the story the religious instinct.

Most humans who admit the existence of God fall into two camps: those who believe God is a Someone, and those who believe it is Something. Those who say God is an impersonal "Force," see behind all created things the "awful shadow of some unseen power."

This power, however, remains vague; not because it *is* vague, but because it is far beyond anything we can imagine. All religions agree that God is greater than anything our minds can conceive. All agree that God is the energy source for all life, but some religions prefer to leave it there. The followers of Hinduism,

25

Buddhism, New Age religions, and primitive religions hold to this view. If you like, they think God is a vast form of focused energy.

"The Force" is an excellent name for this Divine-power because you can think of it like electricity. This "Force" or "Energy" drives all things and holds all things together, but in the end it is an impersonal force. Like electricity, It doesn't have a particular mind or a will.

Beyond Good and Evil

A "Life Force" *does* seem to surge through all creation, and if God is simply the "Life Force" then it would explain why all the different religions seem to be headed in the same basic direction. For Christians, Jews, and Muslims also believe that God is the source and energy force of creation. This idea of God, then, seems like a simple one that would solve all our problems and differences.

But if God is *only* "The Life Force," this raises more problems than it solves.

First of all, if God is merely the "Life Force" then that force (because it has no personality) must be indifferent to what we call good and evil.

This is easy enough to understand if you think of the "Life Force" as electricity. Is electricity good or evil? It seems good when it lights your desk but it seems evil when it electrocutes your grandma. Electricity itself is neither good nor evil. In the same way, if what we call

26

God is just the "Life Force," then it is neither good nor evil. It can't decide anything one way or another.

If this "Life Force" is impersonal and has nothing to do with good and evil, then our ideas of "good" and "evil" must be an illusion. Some people believe this. They say a particular thing is only good or evil depending on your point of view. Good is what helps you to survive. Evil is what hurts you.

Are good and evil only useful illusions? I don't think so. The human sense of right and wrong is about more than just what happens to be pleasant for us or helps us survive. For example, what we consider to be good is often not pleasant. Being good is not easy. I would rather sit home and watch TV and eat potato chips than go and visit my irritable, but lonely neighbor. I would rather play video games than learn to play the piano.

Furthermore, what we consider to be the highest good is often the most unpleasant thing of all, and it doesn't help us survive. It does the opposite. If I die for my country or become disabled because I rescued a drowning child, everyone will think it "good" even though, for me as an individual, it is not good.

Good and evil, then, are greater than what happens to be pleasant or helpful to us or unpleasant and hurtful. There seems to be a standard for what is good and evil which is greater than us. Because of this, people have concluded that there is some other source of good and evil that is above and beyond our basic needs and desires. This source of good and evil exists as a constant—always presenting us with a choice.

"Here is something good" that source of good and evil seems to say, "will you choose what is good?"

Does the Force have a Face?

For good and evil to exist there has to be such a thing as choice. In other words, an action can only be good or evil if we have chosen it. If we had no choice in our lives; if we simply did what we are programmed to do by our genetic history or by our upbringing, then there could be no such thing as good and evil. We'd be simply acting out a destiny that had already been determined for us.

However, each of us has a mind and a free will. We can "go with the Force" or "turn to the dark side." Where did this power to choose come from?

If the "Life Force" were just energy and not a person, then it could not be the source of goodness and it could not be the source for beings like us who have minds and free will. Could the "Life Force" be inferior to the beings it created? Could an energy force without a mind and will be the source for good and evil? Could a mindless energy force create beings with minds and wills? If so, how would the "Life Force" have thought of such beings in the first place?

However, if the "Life Force" also has a mind and a will, then in some sense it has personality. Therefore, Jews, Christians, and Muslims conclude that God is more than just the "Life Force." We say that God is *personal.* In other words, the Force has a Face.

Is God Good?

As soon as we say, "God is personal" we don't mean that God is just a great big, old man with a white beard who happens to live on a cloud in the sky beyond space and time. What we mean is, instead of saying he is the "Force" of creation, we say he has an individual mind and will; that he is the Mind and Will by whom all things were created, and by whom all things live and move and have their being.

God is therefore not just a force, but he can make a choice, and because he can choose he must therefore be either good or evil. Christians, Jews and Muslims believe he is all-good.

Can God truly be all-powerful, and all-good? Now we have come to that most troublesome and intriguing question.

If this personal God we've discovered is all-powerful and all-good why does He allow evil? If he were all-good he would want to stop evil from happening, and if he were all-powerful he would be able to do what he wants. It is easy to conclude therefore, that if there is a God he can't be both all-good and all-powerful.

Some religious systems get around this problem by proposing that there are two powerful forces: a good force and a bad force. This is called Dualism. Another form of Dualism teaches that God holds within himself both the good and the evil, and that evil is simply the "shadow side" of God of the force, and that sounds like Obi Wan's religion.

When you think it through, neither of these views really hold up. If God had a good side and a bad side like we do, or if there were two forces in the universe; one for good and the other for evil, then those two opposing forces would always be battling for supremacy.

This theory sounds like the way the world really is, but there is a problem with it. For there to be two opposing forces, (one good and the other evil) there has to be some other power greater than the two forces that decides what is good and what is evil, otherwise the battle between good and evil would be meaningless.

Evil is Good Twisted

Furthermore, when you examine good and evil you find that they are not equal. This is because of the nature of evil itself. Think for a minute. Have you ever noticed that there is nothing original about evil? Every type of evil is only a good thing twisted and deformed.

This applies to any evil action from the tiniest lie to the most monstrous crime. So a lie is nothing positive in itself. It is the absence of truth or else it is the truth twisted. Likewise every crime is something good twisted. As darkness is the absence of light, and cold is the absence of heat, so evil is not something positive. It is the absence of good or something good distorted.

That makes it sound like evil isn't so bad, or that evil is not real. Evil is real, but its reality is rooted in the reality of goodness. Evil is bad not only because it is the absence of good, or something good distorted, but also because it is parasitic. Evil feeds on the good, and like any parasite, it actively destroys its host. Evil takes the good and twists it—sometimes beyond all recognition. Like light and heat "Good" is solid, positive and real. Goodness is also everlastingly beautiful. Evil, on the other hand, is a dark and empty shadow—a force of distortion and destruction. This is why Christians say there cannot be two equal gods—a bad one and a good one.

Christians also say that God cannot have any of that parasitic shadow within himself, because to be the powerful Positive Presence, God must be solid, good and everlasting, not twisted, dark and empty. I realize however, that I still haven't answered the question. If God is all-good and all-powerful, why does he allow evil?

Freedom to Turn to the Dark Side

The answer to the riddle is built into the question. When we say God is all-good and all-powerful we are automatically saying that his goodness and power are very different from ours. In other words, because he can see and know everything, his goodness and power must be of a different order than ours.

If God is all-good, then when he creates something he cannot help but create it perfectly. Because God is all-good and all-powerful he created everything, including human beings, as perfect as they could be. Part of that perfection is that he gave us a mind and will. This is what the old creation story means when it says humans were created in God's image.

Having a mind means we can make decisions, and having free will means that we have the power to act on those decisions. If we have free will, then we have the choice to do good or to do evil.

Indeed, as I tried to show earlier, good and evil don't have any meaning *unless* we have the free will to choose. If you like, as soon as free will existed, so did good and evil. As soon as there was the opportunity to choose between two things, one thing had to seem better to us than the other.

If we didn't have this free will we wouldn't have been created perfect. Could God have created us with free will, but without the ability to choose evil? No. Even God can't do something which is logically impossible.

Would we have been more perfect if we were robots? I doubt it. However, you can see where this leads: if we have free will there is the very real risk—in fact the very real probability—that sooner or later we will use that free will to choose evil. For if God forced us to do only good, then it wouldn't be good because we hadn't chosen it freely.

Having created us with free will, God continues to extend that gift to us today. We can do what we want. It's as simple as that. In theory, God could remove our free will to prevent suffering, but that would turn us into robots, which would make us less than human, and that would not be good. God could prevent the consequences of our bad choices so we would not suffer, but then, we would be like characters in a war video game—engaged in life and death decisions that were unreal.

An all-good God who allows evil actions that lead to suffering, then, is not as difficult as a supposedly all-good God who would turn us into mindless robots. Suffering then, is the price we pay for being like God and having free will.

The Downward Spiral

Choosing evil twists something good, and from that twisted choice comes the vast majority of suffering in the world. It's true that there are other forms of suffering that are not caused by the bad choices of human beings. Natural disasters or birth defects cause huge amounts of human suffering. However, despite the terrible suffering they cause, natural disasters and defects are not evil in themselves. They are merely part of the natural order.

This kind of suffering—seemingly random and without blame—is part of a deeper problem. The violence of the natural world shows us that there is a fault line running through the whole of the created order. Things aren't quite right. The world is broken. Violence, pain and fear seem to be woven into life at a deep level.

Psychologists tell us that some of our illnesses and even many of our accidents are caused by stress, anger, aggression, and violence. The world is more complicated than we imagine, and the causes of all events are inter-related. It may be that in some dark pattern even the natural disasters, birth defects and accidents are part of the negative effects of the bad choices of the whole human race.

That doesn't mean we are all to blame for our own suffering. Often we are the victims of the bad choice of another person. We live in a world that is riddled with hidden horrors—shot through with bad choices and the twisted results of those bad choices. The beauty of the world is darkened by evil, and we're right to question God about this grim fact.

The Price of Freedom

There is an answer, but it is not easy. If all the evil in some mysterious way comes back to the bad choices of the human race, we have to conclude that God must have foreseen all the suffering that would result from our bad choices, and considered it worth the risk.

The answer may not be quite as grim as it sounds. It may be that the suffering, in the long run, teaches us lessons that we could not learn in any other way. Maybe, in some mysterious and terrible way, we are becoming more perfect by going through the evil and coming out the other side, than if we had never gone through it at all. Just as an athlete or a soldier becomes stronger through being strained, exerted, broken down and then rebuilt.

I said the question of suffering was vitally important. It is important because it brings us to the very heart of God and to the very heart of the Christian faith. Some people think Christianity is simply a happy-clappy, schmaltzy religion that skirts around the enormous problem of suffering. Nothing could be further from the truth. As we shall see throughout this book, struggling with the problem of human suffering is precisely what Christianity is all about.

Rather than simply giving an intellectual answer to the problem, the Christian religion is itself the solution to the problem. The answer to the problem of suffering runs through the whole story of Christianity like a scarlet thread in a vast and beautiful tapestry.

If you really want to answer the question of suffering, then you can't be satisfied with mere intellectual answers. Each one of us is stuck in the middle of the problem of suffering, because we all suffer. To really have the answer means getting involved and struggling to work out the problem—not just with our heads, but with our hearts and our whole lives.

This is far from easy, because one of the symptoms and causes of the suffering is the fact that we are confused and cut off from the answer. We are cut off from God. Like wounded, lost children we are in pain and we do not know where to turn. The next thing we have to consider is how God might be trying to wade into our confusion and fear to find us and bring us home.

Chapter Four
Hide and Seek

The ancient story of the Garden of Eden shows us the human condition. God created men and women with free will, but without the knowledge of good and evil. He placed them in a beautiful primeval paradise, and gave them one commandment: they should not taste the fruit from the tree of the knowledge of good and evil.

As the story goes, they used their will to make a bad choice: they disobeyed God's command and ate of the tree. As soon as they chose badly, they *did* have the knowledge of good and evil, and part of that knowledge was that they felt guilty. Their first instinct was to run and hide from God. Suddenly instead of being content in God's presence, they began to fear God and do anything they could to stay away from him.

God, however, was not going to let them go. He came to find them, and asked them what had gone wrong. When they told him, he had to expel them from the Garden of Eden, to wander the earth as exiles. Worst of all, they would have to grow old and die—otherwise they would live in their twisted condition forever.

The ancient religious stories are full of simple wisdom. They can be far richer than intellectual arguments about the existence of God, and about the nature of good and evil. The Garden of Eden story outlines the stark truth about our human condition quite simply. Men and women choose to disobey God's plan for their lives. This makes them suspicious of each other, unsure of themselves and fearful of God.

As a result their instinct is to hide from God. Adam and Eve's expulsion from paradise symbolizes the fact that we all wander in a hard and dangerous land, full of anger, violence, and fear. This is the spiritual condition of the human race. We live in a land of exile, where we are cut off from God, cut off from eternal life, and cut off from real happiness.

Here I Come, Ready or Not

The Garden of Eden story also shows us what God is like. He doesn't wash his hands of Adam and Eve. Although they are hiding, he comes to find them. Even though he expels them from paradise, the later chapters of the Book of Genesis show that God stays with them.

In other words, God does not forsake what he has made. He is always on a search and rescue mission. Like a salvage expert, he goes out and about seeing what can be hauled up, re-cycled, rescued, and restored. He doesn't want us to be lost forever. He wants to straighten out the twist in our character and put us on the road back to Eden.

But God has a problem: we are very good at hiding. Ever since Eden we have learned to run and hide not only in the bushes, but within any bit of cover we can find. Furthermore, part of this inherited twist in our nature is the habit of blaming God for doing the hiding. We realize he is difficult to follow and understand, so we say it's *his* fault, and that he is distant and unconcerned about us.

Wake Up

Not only do we hide from God, but in our hiding place we are fast asleep. Many religions speak of the beginning of the religious quest as "waking up."

If we are to make any progress in our knowledge of God, we first have to wake up. We have to open our eyes and see that God has been there all the time, waiting for us to wake up. Rather than being distant, he has been closer to us than we are to ourselves. Instead of hiding, he has constantly been trying to reveal himself to us.

You may have been following this argument intellectually so far, but if you are going to go any further you will have to "wake up" fully. Now your emotions and will need to be engaged. If you are going to learn more about God you will need his assistance, and to receive this assistance you have to ask for it.

Therefore, right now, take a break from this book. If you

have the courage to do so, ask God to wake you up.

That's right, take a break from this book and say to God, "God, I'm sorry I've been asleep and far from you. If you are there, wake me up! Help me to understand more fully your existence in the world."

Did you do it? Did you mean it? Maybe for the first time you have prayed a real prayer. This is important because at this stage we are going to consider four ways God communicates with us, and if you haven't opened yourself to God through that short prayer you will not really understand the next part of this book.

If God really wants us to be aware of his presence, and learn more about him, how would he make himself known?

There are four basic ways God speaks to us. The four ways all interact with each other, working together to help us see God and understand the way back to harmony and peace with him.

Understanding and accepting the reality of God with our minds is only one aspect of the plan. He also wants us to be involved with our hearts, our wills, and our bodies, to understand who he is and what we should do.

In other words, it is not enough for us to open our eyes and wake up. We also have to get up, get dressed, get washed, and get a new life.

Four Ways to Find God

Observing the world and understanding the reasons for God's existence only takes us so far. We have bodies and emotions as well as an intellect, and since our brains, emotions and bodies work together, it makes sense that God would reveal himself to us through all not only our mind, but our emotions and our physical world.

Therefore, the first way to find God is simply to look around you. The world is his creation, and it tells us what God is like in the same way that a poem, a play, or a painting reveals the personality of the writer or artist. By observing nature we can gather that God has created an ordered and complex world, both beautiful and terrible.

Beauty is Truth and Truth Beauty

We see the world with our eyes, we think about it with our minds and we have emotions about the world. All this combines to make us realize that the world is beautiful.

We have a deep sense that what is beautiful is also deeply true, and what is true always has an air of beauty about it. We often decide what is true and beautiful by relating it back to nature. The more natural a thing is, the more we consider it to be true and beautiful. So, although we might like silk flowers, real roses will win every time. That is because real roses are both truer and more beautiful than silk roses.

Our sense of beauty then, points us to truth, and this unlocks another secret of God's personality. The world he has created has an inner logic, simplicity

41

and unity that we look to as a model for all that is beautiful and true.

We may disagree about the relative beauty in the world around us. You might like beaches while I love rugged mountains. Furthermore there is a whole second level of beauty and truth created when human beings make things. Yet each form of beauty and truth from music and drama to poetry and paintings points us to a beauty and truth that are beyond and above this earthly realm.

The beauty and truth we see around us are not infallible pointers to God but they do reveal more of what God is like. So we conclude that God is the source of a beauty and truth, and that if this is so he must have that simplicity, unity, and beauty to an overwhelming degree.

The Good, the Bad, and the Ugly

The sense of beauty and truth help us to discern what God is like, but along with this instinct for beauty and truth we also have a sense of right and wrong. People may not agree on the details, but they all agree that there is such a thing as right behavior and wrong behavior. For example, some people may think it is all right to have ten wives. Others think you must only have one. But almost all agree that you mustn't sleep with another man's wife.

Our moral instinct is another pointer to God's personality. Since we all have this general sense of right and wrong, God must be the ultimate source of what is right and good.

Just as what is beautiful and true is usually that which is most natural, so also what is most good is also most natural. However, this is the area where we most often make a mistake. Because of our broken human nature, very often what seems natural to us is not always good. So, for example, some people think it is the most natural thing in the world to steal or lie or cheat to further their own ends. Such people have forgotten what is truly natural; confusing it with whatever feels right at the moment. They have slipped into a distorted mindset where they consider un-natural actions and desires to be natural and good.

This kink in our character is what needs correction, and that is why we believe God revealed through the Jewish religion a code of right behavior. This was not to make everyone feel guilty, but to remind everyone what truly natural human behavior *ought* to be. This corrected sense of right and wrong tells us what we ought to be like. It reminds us that we were created in God's image, and to be truly natural and good, we ought to be very different from what we sometimes are.

Furthermore, once we get a glimpse of what we ought to be like we also get a glimpse of what God is like. In other words, when we see how totally natural and good we are meant to be, we can see that God is totally natural and therefore totally good. He is as he should be. He lives in a simple condition in which all that he is and does is good.

God is Love

If God is beautiful, true, and good, then part of that goodness means he is active and outgoing. Goodness is, by its nature, creative, and positive. Goodness does not stay bottled up, but reaches out to those around it. Therefore God must be actively involved in promoting goodness, truth, and beauty in the world.

The Christian New Testament affirms this by telling us that God is Love.

In other words, at the very core of God's being, is this mysterious power of outgoing goodness, truth and beauty we call "Love".

This is not a sentimental kind of love. This is not a sweet emotion or an erotic sensation. Instead it is a powerful, overwhelming desire for the good of others. It is a passion for the perfection of beauty, truth and goodness. It is an ever-increasing spiral of outgoing dynamic power that reaches out and reconcile all things in its embrace. In other words, God is in a loving relationship with the universe and everything in it.

This love is not only what God does. It is what he *is*.

Logic is useful, but it is *love* that really helps us find our way to God.

Learning about God does not mean simply studying books of theology; it means stepping up into an encounter with him. To learn about God we do not just study beauty, truth, and goodness. We enter into Beauty, Truth, and Goodness. The Old Testament talks about "knowing" God, and the word "knowing" is the same word it uses to describe the intimate relationship between husband and wife. To know God is to "make Love" in a way far more glorious, profound and mysterious way than any human lovers might imagine.

I say this because human love and the Divine Love are connected.

It is through the drama and joy of human love with all its hopes and fears, all its triumphs and tragedies, that we really find, and come to know God.

It is not just in formal religion and intellectual theories about God that we discover God. That only takes us so far. Instead it is in the stories of real people, and their struggles with good and evil, joy and sorrow, love, hatred and forgiveness that we discover God.

This is why religious people speak of religion as an adventure or a quest. While we set out to search for God we discover that all the time he has been searching for us.

Chapter Five

Knowing God

Anyone who has learned to ride a bike knows that we learn better by doing than by being taught the theory of bike riding. Learning to ride a bicycle makes books about bike rides seem irrelevant. It might be easier to read a book about bike rides, but riding a bike is far more real. It is also far more dangerous. Riding a bike involves risks. It means crashes, and grazed knees.

Knowing God is just the same. Although study comes into it, we're talking about an activity, not a spectator sport.

Knowing about God and knowing God are not the same thing.

Knowing God is far more like making friends with a person than learning facts about that person. It is in doing things with a person that we learn most about him, and so it is in living life with God that he reveals himself to us most powerfully. God reveals himself to

47

us through our own relationship with him, but he also reveals himself as we learn about his relationship with other people.

Show Me Don't Tell Me

If God is Love, and if he is best known within a relationship, then you would expect religion to be concerned with stories about God's relationship with people.

Most religions do just that. They tell stories about God's interaction with human beings.

However, the religious stories of the world are not all straightforward. Some of them take the form of myths and legends. They are ancient, imaginative stories about gods, goddesses, and human beings that no one pretends are actually real, historical figures.

These stories are useful, because they reveal the truths of that particular religion. The stories "incarnate" the religious principles and ideas. The word "incarnate" simply means "to put flesh on." The stories of the various religions flesh out the teachings about God.

The Myth of the Hero

The stories from many different religions around the world vary enormously, but there is one type of story that comes up time and time again. The story of the hero's quest arises in almost every culture and at every time down through history from ancient India to the latest Hollywood film.

The story of the hero's quest is simple. The hero is a special person who must leave his home to set out on a great adventure.

Usually the hero is on a quest to find some treasure or rescue a loved one. The outer quest also has an inner meaning. The hero may be looking for a Golden Fleece or a magic sword, but he is also looking for eternal life, spiritual enlightenment, and salvation. To do this he has to overcome great difficulties, defeat a terrible enemy and gain the prize.

The hero's story shows us how to fight life's battles, but it also shows us that we are all on a spiritual quest to find God. The ultimate prize is not just happiness, health, and wealth, but spiritual enlightenment, salvation, and eternal life.

In most religions, the various kinds of myths have no link with history. The stories help people on their own spiritual quest, but everyone knows the hero is not a real person; or if he was real, that the story has been made much more elaborate in order to teach the necessary lessons.

Stories about great heroes crop up in every religion and culture, but there is one religious tradition that is startlingly different. In the Jewish religion, the heroes are all portrayed as real people. They are not magical figures from wonderful fairy-tale stories. Instead they are presented as historical characters who lived in a real relationship with God himself.

As a result, when you read the Book of Genesis in the Old Testament, you find that Abraham traces his ancestry back to Noah, and from Noah to Adam. In other words, the ancient Jewish writers are keen to show that Abraham was a descendent of that first person with whom God had established a special relationship, and if Adam was created in God's image as a son of God, then Adam's descendent Abraham is also part of the same family.

The different world religions tell stories about the gods' relationships with human beings, but in the dusty old stories of the Jewish people those stories come into focus in a historical way. Therefore, to understand how God relates to people, Jews and Christians have told and re-told the marvelous old stories of the Jewish nation.

The Saga of God's Family

The Old Testament is a bit like one of those soap operas about the life and loves of a vast extended family. It is in fact a saga of one family's unique relationship with God. The father of the family was Abraham. He was the chieftain of a nomadic tribe in the Middle East sometime around 2,000 BC. He lived with the great civilizations of Babylon to the East and Egypt to the southwest, and wandered in the territory which is now the nation of Israel and Palestine. In the Book of Genesis God promises Abraham a large family and a rich land, if he would only step out and follow God's lead.

The problem was, Abraham was childless. Then late in their lives, Abraham's wife Sarah bears a son called

Isaac. In a very strange and terrible story, God asks Abraham to sacrifice his son Isaac on a hill called Moriah. As they are going up the mountain the boy asks his father why he had no animal for the sacrifice. Abraham says to his son, "God himself will provide the sacrifice." Then at the last minute God calls from heaven that Abraham should kill a ram instead, and the boy's life is spared.

Hints and Guesses

That disturbing story from the Book of Genesis illustrates another curious fact about the Jewish people. All through the Old Testament we get the impression that they are longing for something greater. They are always looking forward with hope to the promises of God.

No matter how down and out they are, no matter how much they rebelled against God, still they eventually turn back to him. In a rather poignant way, the Jews were a hopeful people. No matter how desperate their situation, they always trust that God will bring them into something better.

The story of Abraham nearly killing his son is one of those strange "pointers" forward. When Abraham says, "God himself will provide a sacrifice" he is getting a glimpse of the future.

These hints and clues to a great, but unknown future are littered throughout the story, so that all through the Old Testament we get the picture that God is laying a plan.

Dwight Longenecker

His secret plan is not only for the Hebrews, but for the whole of the human race.

Slavery and Freedom

In the stories of the Old Testament, God reveals what we human beings are like, and what he is like. This is the marvelous way God speaks—not primarily through a law or theological teachings, but through the drama of one family's roller coaster ride through history.

As the story moves on, Abraham's great-grandson Joseph is sold by his brothers to be a slave in Egypt. Then when a great famine hits the land the brothers travel to Egypt to get food and are saved by the same Joseph, who has now become the Pharaoh's regent and governor of the whole country.

Joseph's brothers settle in Egypt, but several generations later their descendants—the Hebrew people— have become slaves. However, they did not forget the promise of a great nation and a great land.

A fugitive from Egypt, a Hebrew called Moses is summoned by God to go back to Egypt and lead the people to freedom. At that point God promises, "I will raise up from among the people a prophet like you."

Part of Moses' task is to give the people God's law, and to set up a religious system for them to follow. Part of that religious system is a system of animal sacrifice. The other religions of the Middle East had animal (and human) sacrifice, but they sacrificed animals to please angry gods in order to have fair weather and good harvest.

CATHOLICISM / *Pure and Simple*

Moses sets up a system in which sacrifice wins forgiveness for breaking God's law. The theory was that your death penalty for sin would be taken by the animal, and you would be forgiven.

Signs and Symbols.

This sacrificial system is another one of God's hints. The way he takes an already existing religious idea and transforms it is typical of the Old Testament, and it shows us how the different world religions relate to each other.

Time and again God works through the religious genius of the Jews to take a crude way of thinking about God and re-make it to reveal what he was *really* like. For pagan peoples the sacrificial animal was offered as meat for a hungry god to devour. The Jews, under God's guidance take this religious action and find there a more profound and beautiful meaning.

When Moses leads the Hebrews from slavery in Egypt God asks them to sacrifice a perfect lamb. This Passover Lamb (also called the Lamb of God) is killed so that their oldest sons would not die when God sends the angel of death to visit Egypt.

This sacrifice is not performed to please God, but to deliver the Hebrew children from death. The ceremony echoes the sacrifice that Abraham made to deliver *his* son from death.

It also points forward to another Lamb of God, a final sacrifice that would one day deliver all of humanity from death. Eventually the Hebrew people do go into the land that is now Israel, and once they arrive there God chooses a shepherd boy to be their king.

Prophets and Priests

In God's way of using signs, actions, and picture language, the shepherd boy David becomes the symbol of another shepherd King who would one day come to rule his people.

In the whole history of the Jewish people God gradually reveals himself. He doesn't simply tell them what he is like. Instead he is there with them, as a father is with his child, walking beside them and teaching by showing and doing rather than by telling.

In this way the truth of who God is and what he is like was being lived out within history. God reveals his character to them within their experience as a nation, as individual families, and as individual people. We can see that it is God's way to reveal himself within the very fabric of life.

The Jewish religious system was maintained by priests who were drawn from a special tribe of men. The priests conducted the religious rituals for the people. The priests also instructed the people in the religion and kept the whole system going, just as priests and clergy do today.

However, there was another breed of religious leaders who were not quite so humdrum and part of the establishment. The prophets were men who were inspired by God to preach to the people. They stirred the people up with dramatic actions, radical preaching and an uncompromising message. The message was that God loved his people. He was unhappy that they continually turned away from his ways and he called them time and again to return to friendship and fellowship with him.

The Return of the King

David, the King of the Hebrews lived around 1,000 BC. His son Solomon would build up the family dynasty to a point of great power and glory, but within 500 years the kingdom falls and the people are taken into exile. Nevertheless, the prophets tell them not to give up hope. God will bring them back to the land and one day a new son of David will be their king.

God sends various prophets to look forward to the coming of the King in different ways. One says that God will be the Shepherd of his people, then that the coming King will also be the Shepherd of his people.

Another says that a virgin will give birth to a child who will be called, "Emmanuel"—which means "God is With Us." The prophet Isaiah says that this promised one will be the "Servant of God" and that he will end up suffering terribly to redeem the people.

The prophet Daniel has a vision in which he sees "one like the Son of Man" sitting at God's right hand. This "Son of Man" is one who appears like a human being, and yet has the glory and majesty and power of God.

For 2,000 years, from the time of Abraham onward, God works in a unique way in the history of the Jews. They are a chosen race, not because they are superior somehow, but because they have a unique faith.

This faith doesn't make them perfect. Their history is one of spectacular failures and disastrous choices. Despite their failings, they are God's people, and through them he works out his plan for the whole human race.

Through the Jews God promises a new king—a chosen one—one anointed to bring in an everlasting kingdom of peace and justice for all. The prophecies about this king are mysterious, but they are clear that he will be unique, and that he will come to perform a special function in the world.

By the time of the Roman Empire the Jews have returned to their land and are looking forward to the promised king.

At this point in history God's revelation of himself comes to a climax point. The time of hints and guesses, signs and symbols, ends, and the ultimate revelation of God is about to burst in upon human history.

SECTION TWO

THE GOD MAN

Chapter One
The Ultimate Revelation

The Blind Leading the Blind

If you were God, what would you do? You created men and women to be your sons and daughters. You wanted them to be part of your family; you wanted them to be happy, but they turned away from you. In turning away from you their human nature became twisted. Suddenly their instinct was to hide from you.

They wanted to hide for two reasons. First, they assumed you were angry with them, and they were afraid. Second, something inside of them whispered that it would be far more interesting to do things their own way.

This is what Christians mean by "original sin." When we say a baby is born with original sin, we're not saying that the baby is terribly and totally wicked. We are simply acknowledging that the baby, like every one of us, came into the world with a defect. He was born wounded.

CATHOLICISM / *Pure and Simple*

Likewise, when Christians say that every human being is a sinner, we are not saying that everyone is totally and utterly evil. Instead we are admitting the fact that, while everyone is created in the image of God, this perfect image is wounded by selfishness, violence, and greed. In other words, our goodness is soiled, and we need a good scrub.

This is common sense isn't it? When we look in the mirror, or when we look at other people, we see human beings who are basically good. However, in each of us there is also a shadow side. In some people the rottenness has spread and they have become more bad than good. But most of us mean well. At heart we desire what is good and true.

Original sin does not mean that we are rotten to the core. It means at a very basic level we are cut off from God. Instead of running towards him we are running away. Instead of looking for him we are hiding from him. One of the results of our hiding from God is that we can't see him clearly. In fact, without his help, we can't see him at all. We're all in this fix together – the blind leading the blind.

So What Would You Do?

Since we all have this flaw in our character we have trouble seeing what is best for us. This flaw makes us tend towards selfish choices. Despite receiving good advice from wise and holy people, we make wrong choices. The situation is similar to that of a family where loving parents have to deal with a rebellious teenager. The parents know what is best, but their good will is met with sullen behavior. To their great sorrow, the parents watch their teenager constantly reject all that is best for him, leading to disastrous decisions. This is why the stories in the first part of the Bible (the Old Testament), which tell of the relationship between the Jewish people and God, are so interesting: not because they give us a beautiful new religion or because the Jewish people are the perfect followers of a spiritual form of life. Instead, the stories capture our imagination because they are a catalogue of human disasters. The heroes of the Old Testament are real people. They are flawed by original sin. Time and again the Jewish people mess up. They reject God; they disregard his law and wind up as miserable failures.

Another consequence of original sin is that people instinctively feel guilty and afraid of God. Because their instinct was to fear God, the people of the Old Testament sometimes perceived God as being angry with his people. It is true that sometimes the Old Testament God comes across as angry and vengeful, but more often he is shown to be patient and forgiving. An ancient Jewish poet says God is "slow to anger and rich in mercy." And through the voice of the Old Testament preachers, God cries out, "Oh, my people, what have I done to you? What have I done to make you turn away from me?"

God sees that we are like sheep without a shepherd. We long for happiness, and we are searching everywhere to find it. At the same time, God sees that we are running from the very source of happiness, which is himself. But how can God get through to us if there is a part of us that instinctively runs and hides from him? How can God reveal himself to us, if our eyes are shut tight? What would you do?

Getting Through

First of all, God made sure that a hunger for goodness remained within each one of us. Because God made us, no matter who we are there will always be a part of us that searches for God—even if we think we are only searching for happiness. This is where the religious instinct in humans comes from. In fact, it is so strong that we are looking for God even when we think we are running away from him.

When we desire something beautiful, deep down we are searching for God, the source of beauty. Our desire for youth, and our fear of death and old age is really our desire for eternal life, and that too is a desire for God. When we want what is good and true, or when we cry out for justice, we are expressing our desire for God. In all these ways, at the very depth of our being, we long for God. We can't help it. It is written into our nature. That's how we're wired.

However, our natural search for God can only take us so far. Remember, there is a flaw in our nature, so that while we long for God, we also turn away from him. In a similar way we want beauty, truth, goodness, and justice, but that which is totally beautiful, true, just and good also seems severe and threatening. We long for love, and yet we are frightened of being consumed by the very love we long for.

Making a Prophet

In the second part of the Old Testament the Jewish writers begin to speak the language of love. The prophets were holy men who taught the Jewish people about God in a vivid and powerful way. In many different ways the Jewish prophets tell us that God loves his people.

They say God is like a passionate lover who seeks and pursues the beloved everywhere. He is a faithful husband who loves his wife no matter what she does. The ancient Jewish writers tell us that God is a good and gentle shepherd. He is a wise and gracious king, a patient Father, and a long-suffering servant. The prophets say that he is a faithful God: although we might turn away from him, he will never turn away from us.

Out of all these images of love, one image came into focus. First and foremost God reveals that he is a loving *father*. In a way then, his love is like human love. Yet it is so far greater that it is not like our human love at all. Our love is always mixed up with false motives, fantasy, and selfishness. But God's love is totally pure and real. It is never selfish. It does not love others because it wants to be loved itself. Instead it loves others simply for who they are. God's real love is unconditional. It is also active. It takes the initiative. It reaches out, and draws the loved one into an everlasting embrace.

The Author Steps on Stage

Real love is also *sacrificial*. If you really love something or someone, you will even go through pain and suffering for that person. All along we had thought God was the stern judge, a distant creator, or a vengeful tyrant; but instead God is like this: he is a vulnerable and faithful Father.

By giving us freedom to choose, God subjects himself to our will. In allowing us to run away from him, God allows himself to be rejected and despised. This is a shock. It upsets all our expectations and prejudices. It is so surprising that no wonder it took 2,000 years for such an astounding truth to sink in.

The message of the Old Testament prophets was that God's love for his people was so great, that he would continue to reach out despite their continual rejection. To do this he planned to send a messenger who would communicate his love in a new and unforgettable way.

We can communicate with our loved ones with letters, cards, and gifts. But in the end we want to come and be with them. We want to speak to them face-to-face. This is what God chose to do. All the symbols and signs pointed to this end: God would come and visit his people.

The earlier Jewish writers said God was like a shepherd and a king, but the later writers said the Shepherd King would appear. When the Jewish people escaped from slavery they sacrificed an innocent lamb, but their later prophets said the sacrificial Lamb of God would come to them in a startling way.

They would no longer have to interpret vague prophecies and learn about God's love through religious writings. There would be no need to read about him in signs and symbols because all the symbols were about to be shown clearly. There was no need to read a biography; because the subject of the book was about to enter the room. The time for stories and plays were over, because the author was about to step on to the stage.

Chapter Two
Mother and Child

God's Secret Plan

Throughout the history of the Jewish people, God was setting the stage. First of all he was showing that he is not a distant deity, but a God who is involved with real people at real places in real time. The saga of the Jewish nation "incarnated" God; it fleshed out God's character so we could understand (by his actions) what he was really like.

But the Old Testament story with its symbols and signs of promise also pointed to a more powerful incarnation of God yet to come.

Adam had been created in the image of God, but that image was wounded when he chose his own way instead of God's way. One of the consequences of the bad choice was that, from then on, human beings faced suffering and death.

65

To rescue humans from this curse of suffering and death, and to restore the divine image in them, God himself planned to take human form and secretly enter the world to put things right. Where Adam the human had got things wrong, God would himself become human and put them right.

Christians believe that God took human form the way all of us do—born as a baby of a human mother. But how could God take human form when all human beings carried that fatal flaw in their nature that we call original sin?

To solve the problem God intervened in a unique way when a little girl was conceived. When two ordinary people called Anna and Joachim made love, God made sure that the child who was conceived was free from the distortion of original sin. This baby girl was unique among all human beings, and she is known to us as Mary, the mother of Jesus.

Mary was kept free from original sin for two reasons. First of all, God's human form had to be as fresh and perfect as Adam's had been. Second, a free choice had to be made. God couldn't force himself on Mary. She could only bear God's human form into the world by saying "Yes" to God.

An Amazing "Yes"

Remember, one of the symptoms of original sin is that we instinctively choose the wrong way. The twist in our nature means we have a built in tendency to say "no" to God. Because of this we are not wholly free; we have a bias towards choosing wrongly. For Mary's choice to be really free, her will had to be free of this bias. This didn't mean she would automatically say "yes" to God. It simply meant that she had total freedom to choose without the built-in bias and fear that comes with original sin.

Mary's perfection doesn't mean she was some kind of superwoman. In fact she was very ordinary. To understand this kind of perfection we need to think of something that is perfectly natural, like a forest. When you are in the forest it is beautiful and whole. Everything is working as it should work. However, that perfection seems ordinary because it is natural, and what is natural is not unusual. We don't exclaim with surprise when the sun comes up or when water runs downhill. In that same natural and wholesome way Mary was perfect. She didn't have the flaws and distortions of character that everyone else has. She was simply all that a human woman should be.

Because of the special natural perfection that God gave her, an angel of God recognized that Mary was "full of grace." Grace is another word for the goodness of God, so we believe that this ordinary Jewish girl, was full of God's goodness. Because she was full of God's goodness she could perfectly co-operate with God when he asked if she would be willing to conceive and bear his Son into the world.

This fullness of goodness did not take away Mary's free will and independence. God's grace did not mean

Mary was God's robot. Far from it. Instead this full-ness of God's grace meant that Mary was fully human and fully free. She could have said "no" to God when he asked her to give everything, but at that crucial moment of freedom Mary said "yes."

Son of God and Son of Man

Christians believe that Mary remained a virgin as she conceived and gave birth to Jesus. Jesus didn't have an earthly father. Instead, by a unique miracle, Mary became pregnant by the power of God.

When Mary said "yes" to God she became pregnant, and God took real human form in the little boy Mary named "Jesus." The name "Jesus" was an ordinary Jewish name from that time period, but the name also means "God saves." Christians believe that this Jesus was at once totally God and totally human: not some mixture of the two, not a God in human skin or merely a wise and powerful man. Because Jesus is God in human form we say rightly that Mary is "the Mother of God."

Now if you have been thinking this through at all, you should be saying, "Whoa! Are you expecting me to swallow this?!" You really think God took human form? You believe Mary became pregnant by God? That's mind blowing!" You're right. These claims for Jesus are astounding. The miracles surrounding Mary's life and Jesus' birth are not easy to believe. But stay with it. Remember, the people who lived in Jesus' time didn't find it easy to believe either, and yet certain events occurred to make them see that these conclusions were really the only possible ones to come to.

Are Miracles Possible?

Most any sensible person would step back with disbelief at the idea that God took human form in Jesus Christ.

Did this incredible miracle really happen? To decide whether this is possible or not we first have to ask whether we believe miracles are possible or not. If we conclude that miracles are possible, then we have to ask whether this *particular* miracle could have happened.

As to the first question, there are really only two choices. The first choice is that the universe we live in is closed; that it operates by set laws of nature that never change. If this is so, then everything can be understood by scientific observation. If the universe we live in is closed, then miracles simply cannot happen.

The other choice is that the universe is open-ended. In other words, although there are set laws of nature, the God of nature can suspend those laws if he has good reason.

Which choice is more likely to be the right one? If we believe there is a God who exists above and beyond nature, and he created the natural laws, then we have to conclude (at least in theory) that God can work beyond the limits of those laws, and therefore what we call miracles can happen.

Un-Natural and Super-Natural

Miracles are possible, *impossibilities* are not. In other words, God may produce a miracle, but even he cannot do something that is logically impossible. He cannot make a circle square. He cannot make two plus two equal seven. A miracle, therefore, is not something that goes against nature. It is a unique and unexpected action that happens within nature.

We may wonder, for instance, how Jesus turned water into wine, as the Bible reports. Yet in the natural cycle of things water turns into wine all the time. Rainwater falls and is drawn up into vines that produce grapes that are pressed into wine. Jesus' miracle didn't change nature. It simply speeded things up. How did Jesus walk on water? Walking on water is not an eternal impossibility. We can all walk on water when it's frozen. Jesus didn't suspend or contradict nature; he simply shifted the way it normally works.

The same is true when we think about the miraculous conception of Mary without sin. This unique event does not go against the law of nature. It is not un-natural for a person to be sinless. Indeed, that is our perfectly natural condition. That's how we were first made. When God intervened to make sure Mary had no human flaw he was not doing something un-natural, but restoring what was most natural.

Likewise when Mary conceived Jesus without having made love to a man, God was not doing something totally un-natural or contrary to the laws of nature.

Young women get pregnant. What *would* have been un-natural would be for Joseph to have got pregnant. So what happened to Mary was not un-natural. It was super-natural. In other words, a power greater than nature did something natural in a unique and unexpected way.

This is the kind of miracle we are talking about. Because he created the natural world, God has the power to intervene in that world. We believe that in order to further his plan for the world, God took a few unique actions within nature, over the course of history.

Science and Science Fiction

Despite my explanations you wouldn't be a sensible person unless you still found it all too much to take. God comes down to earth and takes human form? An ordinary girl becomes pregnant with God's son? It sounds like a little bit like a science-fiction story, doesn't it? Where did the Christians get such a far-fetched idea in the first place?

I said earlier that they came to these astounding conclusions because of the rest of Jesus' life. Jesus came on the scene just like any other traveling Jewish preacher. In his time there were other preachers who healed people and gathered crowds around them. There were other religious leaders who had little bands of followers.

Indeed, throughout the world both before and after Jesus there have been many religious leaders who have spoken for God. In most cases their followers don't claim that they were God in human form. And yet, within a few years of his death, Jesus' disciples were teaching quite clearly that Jesus was indeed the Son of God, and that his mother was a virgin, and that he was born as the result of a miracle. How did the followers of Jesus come up with such astonishing ideas?

They came to their conclusions because of what Jesus said and did during his earthly ministry.

Jesus' disciples were Jewish, and as they examined his life in the light of the Old Testament story they came to the conclusion that he really was the Son of God. It was an astounding thing to believe and preach, and to understand why they came to that conclusion we have to look more closely at what Jesus said and did while he was on earth.

Chapter Three
Actions Speak Louder Than Words

John the Baptizer

In the Old Testament, the prophets were traveling preachers who spoke the word of God. But these preachers were also actors. They communicated by their actions as well as their words. For example, one of the prophets named Hosea married a prostitute and was faithful to her even though she carried on with lots of other men. Through his own experience Hosea was trying to drive home the point that God was like a faithful husband and the people of Israel were like an unfaithful wife.

As part of his plan for the world, God prepared Jesus' cousin for a special ministry. This man's name was John and he was called "the Baptizer" because he called the Jewish people to turn away from their selfish ways and return to God. As a sign of their new inwardly clean condition he asked them to be publicly washed with

73

water. This ceremonial washing was called "baptism" from the Greek word *baptizo* which means "to wash."

Like Hosea, John was preaching with his actions as well as his words. He wore rough clothes and lived in the desert as a sign of how terrible it was for people to live in the lonely wilderness of a life without God. To go out into the desert and be plunged into the fresh water was a sign that the person wanted to leave the desert of his sinful condition and enter a fresh, new kind of life.

But John's baptism also echoed an Old Testament ceremony. When the Old Testament king took his throne, the priest anointed him for his new role. The anointing ceremony was the public proclamation of the king's identity and duty in the community.

The prophets were also anointed by God for their ministry. Oil poured on the head of the king or a prophet symbolized the blessing of God flowing down from heaven. This blessing was a recognition from heaven, and a gift of power to enable the prophet or king to perform his duties.

Christ—The Lamb of God

The greatest king of the Old Testament was the shepherd boy, David. After his royal line came to an end, the prophets predicted that one day a new descendent of David would come and assume the throne. He would be a new kind of shepherd king. Because this king was specially chosen by God he would have to be anointed as a sign of his special calling. The Hebrew term for the "anointed one" was "Messiah"; in Greek the word is *Christos*, from which we get the word "Christ."

Once Jesus had grown up we are told that he went out to the wilderness to see his cousin John preaching. John had been telling the people that someone greater was about to appear on the scene. The people were full of excitement and expectation. When Jesus appeared John pointed to him and said, "Behold the Lamb of God!"

Remember, the people considered John to be a prophet—a special messenger from God himself. When he pointed to Jesus and said "Behold the Lamb of God!" the people in the crowd understood that he was referring to the Old Testament stories. The lamb that was killed in the Passover feast was also called "the Lamb of God." That lamb symbolically saved the people from death, and here was John saying that this unknown preacher called Jesus was the "Lamb of God." What could it mean?

Jesus then went to John to be baptized. When John poured the water on Jesus' head it symbolized the anointing of the promised King. To validate the anointing, John heard a voice from heaven saying "This is my beloved Son in whom I am well pleased." Later on Jesus was given the name "Christ" because his followers remembered how his baptism was a kind of anointing by John. When John anointed Jesus he was recognizing that Jesus was the specially chosen Son of David who would be king. He was also recognizing

Jesus to be a specially blessed prophet and teacher. By calling him "the Lamb of God" he was also pointing to another, more mysterious dimension to Jesus' destiny.

Jesus the Good Teacher

Most everyone will agree that Jesus was a great religious teacher. As such he ranks among the other great religious teachers in the world. Many of the things Jesus said are echoed in the words of other religious teachers. But while there are some similarities, there are also some big differences. Other religious teachers give their followers a plan or method to reach God. They teach a technique of prayer, or they teach their followers to obey a system of religious law, or they teach a combination of both.

Jesus also teaches his followers to pray. However, his teaching on prayer is very simple. He doesn't teach difficult meditation techniques. He doesn't require you to undertake a course of study to master complicated religious language. Instead he teaches his followers to speak with God as a child speaks to his father.

Jesus also gives his followers a new kind of religious law, unlike any other religious system of do's and don'ts. It is the law of love. He tells his followers to forgive their enemies, and to love those who do them harm. Jesus sums up all previous laws with two simple principles. First, love God. Second, love your neighbor as yourself. He says that all the religious laws in the world boil down to these two simple principles.

Jesus' teaching was so fresh and revolutionary that it turned the Jewish world upside down. But the most important thing about his religious teachings is not their wisdom and simple freshness, but what they reveal about Jesus himself.

Jesus the Storyteller

One of the most famous ways Jesus taught people was with stories. The stories he told are called parables, and they are a unique form of story. Parables do several things at once. They help people see how to live better lives. They show people what God is like, and like the rest of his teaching, they reveal who Jesus really is.

So, for example, Jesus told a series of stories about the final judgment. In one story a rich man gives various servants some money and asks them to invest it wisely. When later he asks for the money back the various servants have to answer for what they've done, and their responses vary from the brilliant investor to the fool who made no profit at all.

In the story we see how to live wisely, but we also gain insight into God's character—for he is the one who gives the gifts for us to use. And the story also helps reveal who Jesus is, because elsewhere he tells another story about the final judgment, and there he is a shepherd judging between the sheep and the goats. (In Jesus' culture sheep and goats looked very similar so judgment was difficult) Taken together, those two of Jesus' stories reveal him as one who gives us gifts and the one who judges how we have used them.

Lost and Found

Jesus also told a series of stories about things that were lost. A woman loses a valuable coin, a shepherd loses a sheep, or a father loses a runaway son. In each story the person who loses something precious searches relentlessly or waits patiently, and when it is restored there is great rejoicing all around.

The stories teach us to treasure the precious things in life, but they also show us a God who never tires in his search for his lost children. And then when Jesus says he is one who comes to "seek and to save that which was lost" the stories take on a new level of meaning, and point to his real identity.

The story where these different levels of meaning come together most powerfully is the story of the Good Shepherd who goes out to search for his lost sheep. The shepherd has one hundred sheep, but as he counts them at the end of the day one is missing. He goes out into the wilderness to find the lost sheep and brings him home on his shoulders.

In the Old Testament the prophets had said that God was the Good Shepherd of his people, so the story confirms what God is like. But then Jesus says something that his hearers would have found shocking. He calls *himself* the Good Shepherd. In other words, Jesus is saying that the old promise that God himself would be the shepherd of his people is fulfilled in him.

Listen To My Actions

Jesus taught his disciples to pray. He taught them to love God. He told them stories about life. In all these ways he was also showing them who he really was. Like the prophets before him, Jesus not only taught through his words, but through his actions. In what he said and what he did, Jesus pointed to the mystery of his true identity.

In this vein, the miracles of Jesus are not simply the party tricks of an amazing preacher. Neither are they just Jesus' way to show that he had great power. Instead, the miracles of Jesus have a deeper meaning. They reveal not simply that he is a miracle worker. They also reveal who the miracle worker really is.

When Jesus taught the people, they were amazed and said, "This man teaches with authority!" Jesus didn't disagree with them. Instead he said that his authority had been given by God himself. When Jesus healed people from sickness, he also forgave their sins. His enemies were shocked. They said, "only God can forgive sins!" By forgiving people their sins Jesus was making an astounding claim for himself.

When Jesus walked on the water and calmed the storm he revealed who he really was. The Old Testament had said that the Lord God was he "who walks on the waves of the deep," so when Jesus walked on the waves he was revealing that he was none other than the Lord of Creation.

It is true that Jesus was a good religious teacher, but his teachings and actions led his followers to conclude that he was more than just another religious teacher. Who was this religious teacher who had the nerve to forgive sins, calm the storm, heal the sick and perform miracles to feed the hungry?

Jesus the Son of God

Through his stories, his teachings, and his actions, Jesus makes it clear that our relationship with God should be like that of a child with his Father.

But Jesus does more than teach us that we should be the children of God. In all his words and actions Jesus reveals what this new child-Father relationship with God should be like. Furthermore, through his words and actions Jesus is telling us that he is not just *like* God's son. He *is* the Son of God.

We might accept it if Jesus had said, "My relationship with God is like that of a son to his father," but he goes further than that. He says, "I have come to do the will of my father in heaven." And "all authority on heaven and earth has been given to me."

This is where the teaching of Jesus is difficult. There are many people who think Jesus is a good teacher, but they pick out the nice and acceptable parts of Jesus' teaching and sidestep the parts of his teaching that are strange and disturbing. In his stories and in his actions Jesus says that he and God are one. He says this in many ways, but finally he states it quite clearly. He not only says, "I have come to do the will of my Father." He says, "when you have seen me you have seen the Father," and, "I and the Father are one."

Chapter Four
Who is This Man?

The Mystery Man

We wouldn't mind if Jesus were just a good religious teacher. We can accept his teachings about prayer and loving our neighbor. But can we really accept his claims to be the Son of God? We can accept that he was a good person; perhaps the greatest person who over lived. But can we really believe that he is God in human form?

Let's stop and consider for a moment. What kind of person was Jesus Christ? If you want to know, you should sit down sometime and read through one of the gospels in one sitting. I guarantee that the Jesus you meet will be very different from the Jesus you thought you knew.

In the gospels we meet a man who is complex and mysterious, and yet there is no trace of those twists in personality and contradictions of character that everyone else is prone to. He goes through life with a clear purpose and stands out with a majestic simplicity and a quiet intensity that captivates and fascinates us.

He is religious, but never self-righteous. He is pure without being puritanical. He is magnificently good, but never "holier than thou." He is much sterner than the popular image of "gentle Jesus meek and mild." But while he does not tolerate one scrap of evil, he is compassionate towards those who fall into sin. He is shrewd with intelligent people, but simple with more ordinary people. He seems modest, and yet he does miracles and preaches powerfully. He is witty without being sarcastic and gentle without being weak. He is firm without being harsh, self-confident without being proud, and humble without being insecure. In every way he is balanced, mature, wise and sane.

Most importantly, in the gospels we meet someone who is honest and real to his very core. He may be complex, but he is also transparent. There is no trace of guile, self-deceit, or vanity. Jesus is solid and down to earth. He doesn't strike us as a figure out of a story or a play. There is not an artificial or phony bone in his body. Instead he has all the honest unpredictability and complexity of a real person. He knows how the world of power and influence works, but he never schemes or kowtows to anyone. He is his own man, but he is not arrogant eccentric or proud.

When we meet Jesus in the gospels we are confronted with a person who strikes us as being totally complete and whole. Jesus is well-adjusted. He knows who he is. This is what we mean when we say he is perfect. We don't simply mean he never did anything wrong. What we mean is that his personality doesn't have any weakness, faults, or kinks. It is whole and complete. It is all that it should be. Jesus shows us what a totally complete and perfect human being looks like.

The Image of God

If Jesus really was whole and complete in this way, then he was a perfect human being. Yet even though he was perfectly human; he was also fully divine (the New Testament says he is the "image of the unseen God"). However, he did not come to earth like some sort of cosmic superhero. Elsewhere in the Bible it says that although Jesus was in the form of God, "he did not consider equality with God something to cling to, but he took the form of the servant."

The Old Testament prophets pointed to the same truth. The prophet Isaiah said that the Christ would be a suffering *servant*. His purpose on earth was not to receive the accolades and enjoy the dominion that his perfection and divinity deserved, but to serve human beings by suffering for them.

Jesus is the suffering servant, the Good Shepherd, an anointed king, the "Son of Man" who in the vision of the prophet Daniel was as radiant and powerful as God himself sitting on a throne. In a powerful and irresistible way all the symbols and signs from the Old Testament and the New Testament come together like the pieces of a puzzle falling into place. Each sign combines with the others to build up to the conclusion that Jesus Christ's claims about himself may actually be true.

Big Problems

If this is so, then the teachings and life of Jesus present us with some big problems, because all the teachings and actions of Jesus consolidate the claims that he is the Son of God.

Many people believe that "being a Christian" just means following Jesus' commandment to be good. They think it means being kind to others and trying not to lie, cheat, or steal. Of course, Christians should not lie, cheat, or steal, but being a Christian is not simply a case of trying hard to be good. At the very heart of it all, being a Christian means we must come face to face with the astounding claims that Jesus Christ makes.

Put quite simply, Jesus Christ claims to be God in human form. What do we make of that? Presuming that the record we have of his words and deeds is accurate, then logically there are really only four choices.

First, what do we usually think if a person claims to be God? We think he's crazy. Now it is possible that Jesus is crazy, but all the stories we have about him portray him as probably the most same, down to earth and realistic person who ever lived. If those stories are anything close to true, then we can rule out this possibility. The Jesus we meet in the gospels is not a crazy man, whatever else he might be.

The second choice is that Jesus is lying. Again, everything we know about him convinces us that if there was ever anyone honest through and through, this man was. But let us suppose that he *was* a religious fraud. Maybe he was conning everyone. What was his motivation? There is no evidence that he gained either fame or fortune for his fraud. Indeed, he was always trying to escape from the crowds, and we know he lived in total poverty. In the end he gained nothing but pain and a terrible death. Very few frauds will go so far as to die for their lie.

The third choice is that Jesus' followers made a mistake. Perhaps they misunderstood his message. Maybe they thought he was God in human form, but he never intended them to think that.

We'd have to ask whether it is very likely that his followers would come up with such an outrageous suggestion. If they wanted to promote the message of Jesus, wouldn't it have made more sense to describe their friend as a great religious teacher? Once they said he was God, they made him sound not like a great religious teacher but like a madman or a fraud. In other words, even if Jesus did make such a claim, there was every reason for his followers to play it down and turn him into a good teacher instead of the Son of God—a claim that was far more outrageous, dangerous, and difficult to convince others of.

There is one other choice. If Jesus is not a liar, if he is not insane, and if his followers did not make a mistake about his claims then there is only one other choice: he was telling the truth, and he really is who claims to be.

Who Do You Say That I Am?

Jesus didn't allow people much leeway. He said we must make a choice. We are either for him or against him. We cannot serve two masters. We must decide whether or not Jesus really is God in human form.

We would like to defer the decision. We would like to withhold judgment, but by the nature of choice, this is impossible. We must choose, and not to choose is also to make a choice. If you are at a bus stop and a bus comes along you may choose to get on or not. If you say you are not going to choose, then that is a choice not to get on the bus.

When we are making any decision we have to be clear what the choices are. When we read the gospels we have to consider the claims of Jesus. When we do, the option that Jesus was just a good teacher ceases to be viable. As we have seen, he is either God in human form or he is a liar, or he is crazy, or his followers made a terrible mistake. He did not give us the option that he was just a good religious teacher.

Jesus forces this issue for a very important reason. He wants us to understand that another good religious teacher is not what the human race needs. We don't need another system of good works or more techniques of meditation and prayer.

Earlier in the book we raised the difficult problem of suffering. We wrestled with this enormous question of how God can be good yet allow suffering. Jesus under-stood that we need not only an intellectual answer to that question; we need someone to rescue us from the suffering each one of us must endure.

In one of his stories Jesus spoke about the shepherd who goes out on a lonely night to find just one lost sheep. He risks his own life to save that sheep and bring him home safely. When Jesus called himself the Good Shepherd he was saying that this is the reason he came—to seek and to save that which was lost.

Each one of us are like that lost sheep. We're lost in the dark wilderness. Only God can rescue us and put things right, and we can only trust Jesus to help us put things right if we believe that he has the power to do that. The only way he would have the power to rescue us and heal the deep wound at the foundation of our being is if he is God.

The extraordinary claims Jesus made about himself took him right into the very heart of suffering. His claims got him into deep trouble. When Jesus was on trial he faced death because he claimed to be God. The Jewish leaders wouldn't have minded if he were just a good religious leader. They had lots of those. What was one more? What they couldn't stand, was that he claimed to have the power of God. So they killed him. Just as he presented them with a choice, so he presents us with the same choice. And it is a choice between life and death.

Chapter Five
Why Did He Die?

The Problem of Pain

Rather than the end of the story, this is where the story really starts to get interesting. In the first section I said that the question of how a good God could allow suffering was the most important question in the world. I also said that Christianity is the religion that answers the question.

That's because Jesus didn't come to earth simply to give us an intellectual answer to a difficult test question. God didn't take human form in Jesus simply to solve a riddle. Instead, he came to wrestle with the problem at the heart of his very being. In Jesus, God reaches down and embraces the terrible problem of evil and suffering in his own body.

The whole reason for Jesus' existence is summed up in the story of his temptation. After he was baptized by John, Jesus went out into the desert and ate nothing

91

for forty days. While he was in the desert he endured a terrible assault by the devil.

Wrestling With Demons

What do Christians believe about the devil? Satan, or the devil, is a real spiritual being. He is an angel who has fallen from his high condition because he wanted to be like God. Demons are other, lesser angels who have also fallen into the shadow side and seek to pervert God's way in the world.

Satan is also a symbol of death and destruction, violence and mayhem. He stands for the vast range of evil forces arrayed against all that is good. The devil also represents the evil that each one of us struggle against. When he grappled with the devil, Jesus was not just trying hard not to do anything bad. He was beginning a battle with evil that would last for the rest of his life.

His struggle with the devil was a picture of what Jesus' whole life was really about. He did not come simply to teach people about God. He was not on earth just to heal people and teach them how to pray. His main purpose was to answer the problem of evil once and for all—not by teaching about evil, but fighting a terrible battle against the devil, to the very death.

The Unfair Advantage

If a good person decides to fight against evil he will always be at a disadvantage. He is fighting uphill. The good person has to engage with evil. He is not allowed to be a pacifist and sit on one side.

The evil person will naturally use every devious and nasty trick he can think of. That's why he's bad: he is a liar, a cheat, a murderer and a thoroughgoing scoundrel.

However, the good person cannot use the same evil tricks. So the evil one will lie and scheme. He will punch below the belt and throw salt in the good guy's eyes. But the really good person is not allowed to lower himself to dirty tricks. Jesus taught this principle. When our enemy slaps us we are told to turn the other cheek. When our enemy takes our coat we are to offer him our shirt as well.

This disadvantage that the good person suffers is the key that unlocks the whole mystery. You see, evil gets worse and worse in the world when we do not fight it with goodness. We usually respond to suffering by causing more suffering. We seek revenge and return evil for evil.

When we do this, evil breeds in the world and will never be defeated. That is why Jesus teaches us to return good for evil, to forgive our enemies, and pray for those who hurt us. Jesus is trying to get across to us that the only way for evil to be defeated is to smother it with goodness as water puts out a fire.

The Sacrificial Lamb

That sounds neat and tidy. It's not. We forget how evil the enemy really is. If we turn the other cheek and refuse to fight evil with more evil, then by the very nature of that decision we will become victims of evil. Those who are violent will have no qualms about squashing good people under foot. Therefore the stark answer to the problem of evil seems to be that the forces of evil must trample the good person down, and the good person must become an innocent victim.

In the Old Testament religion, this is what the sacrifice of an innocent lamb was supposed to symbolize. The pure little lamb did nothing wrong. He was put forward as symbol of innocence in the face of evil. He was unable to fight against evil, so the evil forces would devour him. He would be slaughtered and die.

When the Jews celebrated their Passover feast in remembrance of their deliverance from slavery, they slaughtered the "Lamb of God" and daubed its blood on their doorways so that the powers of death would pass over their home and they would be delivered. In a symbolic way they believed the innocent lamb took the evil of the world into itself. Evil was absorbed into goodness, even if it meant that the goodness would have to die and the light would have to be put out.

Jesus Lamb of God

All of this is gathered when Jesus takes the title, "Lamb of God." Because he is good, Jesus must battle against evil. But because he is good he is not able to fight evil with evil. He cannot return violence for violence. As a result, the violent will bear him away.

The battle against evil is grim, and the price is great. When Jesus was betrayed by friends, mocked by so called "good" people, condemned by a crooked court and crucified with criminals he shows us that real goodness is devoured by evil. There is no other way. Because the evil one cheats, lies, and uses violence, he wins.

Then at the very darkest and lowest point of the story the tables are turned. The Jewish people celebrated the Passover not as a memorial of defeat, but a celebration of liberation. Through the Passover events they came out of slavery and began their journey to the land of prosperity and promise.

In the same way, when Jesus is trampled down and finally killed by the powers of evil, the tables are turned. Although evil wins the battle, good will win the war.

When faced with the darkest evil we must always remember something that the evil ones always forget: that evil has no real power of itself. Evil is only goodness twisted and perverted. At the heart of evil is a dark void. Because evil is nothing positive in itself it cannot possibly triumph in the end. Likewise, because goodness is positive and powerful, it must finally prevail. Darkness may seem overwhelming, but darkness is nothing in itself. It is simply the absence of light. Therefore even the smallest amount of light must banish the dark.

The powers of evil may have been able to snuff the light of Christ, but they could not put out the light forever. How could evil *really* win? It is impossible because evil (because it is a twisted good) relies on goodness for its very existence. If evil were to win—if the devil could kill God—then he would be cutting off the branch he was sitting on. Because evil is dependent on good for its existence, if good is vanquished, evil itself would also cease to exist.

It was inevitable that Jesus would be trampled by the powers of evil, but he couldn't have stayed dead no matter what his enemies did to him. Because Jesus was God, and because of his overwhelming good-ness, he had to rise again just as surely as the rooster has to crow and just as surely as the sun will rise each morning. Goodness had to prevail. That is the way the whole system is written.

The death and resurrection of Jesus are therefore the ultimate answer to the question of suffering and a good God. Because he is good, God creates a universe where freedom exists. This means evil is a possibility. Evil twists the natural order. It distorts what is good. As a result terrible suffering follows. This suffering goes in a downward spiral away from goodness, away from what is natural, and away from God. But because God is good he himself provides the solution, even though it costs him everything.

A Cause to Celebrate

This is why Christians celebrate Holy Week (including Good Friday, the day on which Jesus died) and Easter as the most important part of the year. Each year we celebrate the fact that Jesus Christ defeated evil not with the tools of evil, but by his overwhelming goodness—even though that meant his own terrible death.

On Easter Day we celebrate the historical fact that Jesus could not stay dead. Death could not hold him. He was too alive, too good, and too powerful for that. His ultimate sacrifice meant that he embraced death and evil and simply squeezed them to death with his overwhelming love and goodness. That's why he rose from the dead, because there was simply no more death to hold him. He was the source of life itself. He could not stay dead any more than water can keep from running downhill.

This is the heart of the Christian faith. To become a Christian we don't just listen to Jesus and try to be good. Instead we come to understand the meaning of his death and resurrection, and we participate in his victory. When people become Christian they accept what Jesus' death means and they are baptized—plunged into water—as a way of plunging into death and resurrection with him.

This is also what Christian worship is all about. We don't go to church just to meet our friends, sing hymns, and hear the good teachings of Jesus. We go to participate in his victory over evil. Through the church ceremony of the *Mass* or the *Eucharist*, Jesus' death and resurrection come alive in the present moment and we re-live them with Christ.

At that point we celebrate the amazing fact that the eternal riddle of evil and a good God has been answered once and for all. The war is over. The victory is won. All that remains is for us to sign the peace treaty and put it into force.

CATHOLICISM / *Pure and Simple*

Chapter Six
What Did He Achieve?

The Second Adam

When the first Christians reflected on the death of
Jesus they came to some revolutionary conclusions.
As Jews, the followers of Jesus considered Adam to
be a representative of the whole human race. The
word "Adam" means "man," so when they said Adam
was created in the image of God the ancient writers
meant all of humanity was created in God's image. If
Jesus really was a new and even fuller image of God in
human form, then it was right to call him (as the Bible
does) "the second Adam."

According to the story, the first Adam brought death
and suffering into the world by his disobedience, but
the second Adam (Jesus) defeated death and suffering
through his total obedience to God's will. The New
Testament says Jesus was obedient "even to death on
the cross." Through his terrible death Jesus wrestled

with suffering and death for the whole human race.

It is difficult for us to put ourselves into the same mindset as these first Christians two thousand years ago. We think individualistically, and find it difficult to understand how one person can represent the whole human race. It's quite sensible to ask, "How can the death of Jesus affect me 2,000 years later?"

In political terms we can all understand how a head of state like a queen or a president can represent the whole nation. Also, scientists tell us that we have all descended from the same genetic parents. In one sense we really are all connected. We are all brothers and sisters in the human race. If this is so, then any human could stand in for the whole human race.

But God didn't choose just any person to represent humanity. He chose the person who was a totally whole and complete and perfect human being. Because he was whole and totally complete as a human being, Jesus Christ held in himself each one of us. So when he embraced suffering and death he really was embracing the suffering and death of each one of us.

Justice and Mercy

Some people find it very difficult to imagine how the death of Jesus can touch us. But there are many ways to think about it. Saying he represents the whole human race is one way. But we can also think about where we were headed, and what it took to turn us around.

Because of our twisted human condition all of us are on the road away from God rather than towards him. This, by its very nature, means we are headed for disaster. It is not so much that God is punishing us because we are naughty little children. Instead, our punishment is built into our decision. Each choice to disobey God has within it the choice to be separated from him forever. If we go our own way we mustn't be surprised if we end up far away from God.

God realizes that we are headed away from him, and he doesn't want us to end up in such a disaster. But because God is good he must also be just. He can't simply take away the natural results of our bad choices, otherwise the choices themselves would be meaningless. So God has to allow justice to take its course.

Because God is good he is not only just—he is also merciful. Therefore God must make sure justice is done while mercy is exercised. So in a brilliant stroke, God has seen fit for his own son to offer the human race both justice and mercy at the same time.

When Jesus died on the cross Christians believe that God himself took the just punishment for our disobedience and offered us mercy in return. It is not that Jesus died in our place to satisfy an angry God. Instead Jesus stepped in to make God's justice effective while he also offered mercy. Part of this mercy means that, if we want to, we can turn away from our selfish path through life, accept what Jesus has done for us and turn back toward God.

Forgiveness Forever

Another way of talking about God's mercy and justice is with the term "forgiveness." We often think of forgiveness as simply excusing somebody for an injury. So when someone steps on our toe we say, "Don't worry, I forgive you."

However, when we are really hurt badly, forgiveness isn't so easy. The person who stepped on our toe didn't mean to hurt us. It was an accident. But if that person steps on our toe not once by accident, but deliberately time and again, then we do not forgive quite so easily. If we do forgive, we are right to demand restitution. If he has broken our toe we might forgive him, but we still want him to pay the doctor's bill.

When Jesus died on the cross Christians believe he won God's forgiveness for all of us. He did this by paying the price of our forgiveness, and that price was the death and suffering that was required for evil to be defeated forever.

Christians therefore say that "Jesus died to save us" or "Jesus died to forgive us." This is what it means in theory, but this is also what it means in reality. The forgiveness and mercy Jesus won on the cross really is available for individual people. The way to obtain this forgiveness is the way we always obtain forgiveness: By asking for it with a sincere heart.

Good, Bad or Forgiven?

This is the simple and astounding truth: Christianity is not foremost about being good. It is about being forgiven. The only precondition for becoming a Christian is not that you be a saint, but a sinner. A Christian comes to realize who Jesus Christ is, and what he has accomplished through his death and resurrection. Once he has realized this, he uses various means to connect with that death and resurrection and claim the results of it for himself.

The simplest way to do this is simply to face facts and say to yourself, "I have been living my life my way. It hasn't brought me real happiness. I want to live life God's way." Once we've come to that realization that we need to tell God so: "Dear God, I want to live life your way. I want to claim forgiveness and mercy from Jesus Christ. Please help me."

At its heart, this is what it means to be a Christian; to hear the call of Christ and decide to follow him. Down through the ages this simple decision has been made by billions of people. Sometimes they have done so with great emotion and felt a huge surge of love and new life in their lives. Other times they have done with quiet confidence and simple trust. However they have done it, these billions of people of every race, language, and tribe down through the ages have simply heard the call of Jesus Christ, and they have dropped what they were doing, turned from their own way and followed him.

Transformed into His Likeness

It is true that Jesus calls us to follow him, but he also says, "you cannot be my follower unless you take up your cross and follow me." In other words, following Jesus means not just trying to live by his teachings, but to imitate his sacrificial actions. Jesus wants us to live in union with him, and to live his life in the world.

This means we are called not just to be religious people, but transformed people. Christians are not just following religious laws and techniques for prayer and meditation in order to be better people. They are seeking to be totally and utterly transformed into the image and likeness of Jesus Christ.

Jesus Christ shows us humanity at its richest and fullest potential. To be like him, therefore, is for each one of us to become all that we can be, and, while remaining ourselves, to be re-created into the image of God—just as God first intended.

This is where forgiveness leads us: to a basic turn-around from walking our own way to walking in God's way. Walking our own way is like a downward spiral into nothingness. Walking God's way is a steady, upward climb into the fullest and richest life imaginable. This climb isn't easy, but it is the goal we were created for, and unless we are on this upward climb we are not becoming all that we can be.

Just as Jesus was the God-Man, so when he calls us to be like him the call is to be no less than God-like men and women. The New Testament puts it another

way. It says our ultimate destiny is to be brothers and
sisters of Christ—the adopted sons and daughters of
God. The exciting news is that he has also given us the
power to accomplish this transformation.

Theory and Practice

This is not just inspiring religious talk. This is not
just theory. It is practice. It can really happen, and this
total transformation of individuals into little god-like
beings is the whole point of the Christian religion. For
this to happen, Jesus Christ established a practical way
for us to become one with him and for this transformation of ourselves, and eventually the whole human
race, to begin.

In order to accomplish this, Jesus did four things.
First he set up a community of like-minded people.
Everyone who wanted to join this community had go
through the ritual of baptism. In this ceremony they
declared their desire to turn from their own way, they
expressed their belief in Christ, and vowed to join his
continuing fight against evil in the world.

Second, Jesus established a basic ceremony through
which this community would always remember his
death, because (as we have seen) his suffering and
death were the heart of the whole matter. Through this
ritual Jesus promised to remain with his followers forever and to fill their lives with his own life and power.

Third, Jesus set up a visible and historical structure for this community. It was simple in its design.

Initially, twelve men would be leaders by Christ's own appointment. As the community grew, they would appoint successors. So they would know who was in charge, Jesus delegated one of those men, named Peter, to stand in his place as the main leader.

Finally, he promised to be with his followers until the end of time. To do this he sent his own spirit into the world to be the Life Force of this fledgling community. The exciting way that Great Holy Spirit transforms our lives and changes the world is the subject of the next chapter.

SECTION THREE

THE FIRE OF LIFE

Chapter One
Jesus Keeps His Promise

You Can't Keep a Good Man Down

Let's not beat around the bush. Christians believe Jesus Christ rose from the dead. We believe this twist in the plot really happened. It wasn't a make-believe happy fairytale ending. It was a real, physical, historical event. It surprised everyone and changed the course of human history forever.

Many people can't believe in Jesus' resurrection and honestly admit they're not Christians. Others want to be Christian, but just can't accept that the resurrection *really* happened. They try to "re-interpret" the resurrection, and say something like, "Jesus didn't physically rise from the dead. Instead, Jesus' *memory* continued to live within the lives of his followers."

This is another way of saying that the resurrection is simply a beautiful idea. But if the resurrection didn't really happen, that idea has no meaning. Its like saying marriage is a beautiful thing, as long as you don't live together or make love. But if you don't live together and make love, then a marriage is not a marriage, and it is not even a beautiful idea, it is no different than friendship.

For marriage to have meaning it has to be physical. Likewise for the resurrection to have meaning, it had to have happened. After all, that's what resurrection *means*: someone rose from the dead never to die again. It's no good just pretending that it was just a beautiful idea. One of the great early Christian leaders, a man named Paul, said that if Jesus didn't truly rise from the dead, then all their faith was in vain.

Did it really happen?

Stop for a moment and think it through. If Jesus Christ really rose from the dead, then it is literally the most important event in human history.

If we want to think about this event fairly, then we must take a serious look at the events recorded in the gospels. Even if the resurrection of Jesus sounds incredible, we must consider the possibility. It is vital to do so because if Jesus did not really rise from the dead, then he was only a good teacher, and if he is only a good teacher he does not have the power to deliver us from death. And if he does not have that power, then he is not the solution to the problem of suffering.

Consider the story: The gospel writers go out of their way to make it clear that the resurrection of Jesus really happened. The gospels were written within the lifetime of eyewitnesses. They report that many people saw Jesus die on the cross and be buried, and that days later the same people saw him walking and talking in their midst.

These eyewitnesses touched Jesus. They saw him eat food. They even put their fingers in his open wounds. Certain details of the story may have altered slightly in the telling, but because eyewitnesses were still living when the gospels were written, we can trust that the gospel writers did not invent the story. Neither did they exaggerate or distort the actual events to any great degree.

When they discovered the empty tomb on Easter morning, Jesus' followers ran away in terror. That shows us just how real, frightening and earth shattering an event this was. Would they have invented such an unbelievable story? In general terms, the more fantastic a story is, the more unlikely it is that people have made it up. The fact that these men and women were later prepared to die for their version of events makes us conclude that something stupendous really did happen to them.

Three Options for the Third Day

What did happen on the third day after Jesus died? There are only three options: The first is that Jesus didn't really die. He just passed out then woke up again. The second option is that he died, but something else happened to his body and they thought he rose again. The third option is that he really did rise from the dead.

Is it possible that Jesus didn't really die on the cross that Friday afternoon? Consider the evidence: Jesus had been whipped by professional torturers to within an inch of his life. Then he was executed by professional executioners who, if they failed, would themselves suffer the death penalty. He had a spear thrust into his side to finish the job.

But let's imagine for a moment that Jesus really did somehow survive the crucifixion. Are we supposed to believe that this man, having been beaten and tortured, having suffered a huge blood loss and terrible wounds would wake up, stark naked, roll back a stone weighing a couple of tons and step out to meet his friends? If they had seen him in such a condition they would have said, "Yikes! Jesus survived—let's get him to a doctor!" Instead they believed that he had risen from the dead.

The second option is that Jesus really died, but something else happened to his body. Maybe a dog ate it or his disciples stole it or his enemies took it. Jews bury their dead immediately and with great respect and care. It's doubtful that something else happened to the body. Are we to believe that the terrified disciples of Jesus suddenly got the courage and brains to come up with a plot to overcome the Roman soldiers guarding the tomb and steal the body away? I doubt it.

When you are examining explanations for seemingly incredible events you must always take the one which is most believable—even if it still seems incredible. So, when you examine the evidence for the resurrection of Jesus Christ from the dead the answer the first Christians gave, and which Christians have believed ever since becomes the only possible solution. It is a solution that is astounding—a solution that turns our world upside down.

A World Turned Upside Down

Jesus' resurrection turned his disciples' world upside down. Once they realized what it meant they were overwhelmed, and we should be too, for the resurrection means that history is changed forever.

Human history is changed because if Jesus rose from the dead, it means that the great enemy, death, can be beaten at last. If the resurrection only means that "Jesus continued to live in the memory of his followers," then victory over death is just a bright idea—no more than religious wishful thinking. If there is no victory over death, then the Christian faith is just another religious system of prayer and good works.

However, if Jesus really rose from the dead, if he conquered evil and death, maybe I can too. Maybe the whole world can be transformed by that same power.

The Christian faith is about that very possibility, and the apostle Paul was so sure of it that he cried out, "Death, where is your sting? Grave, where is your victory?"

Up, Up, and Away

After Jesus rose from the dead he continued to teach his twelve apostles for a time. Then he said that he had to go away, but promised that he would be with them until the end of time. To remain with them he would send a "comforter," the "Spirit of Truth." This Spirit would "lead them into all truth" and "teach them all things." The Spirit of Truth would come to help them, but they needed human leadership too, so Jesus asked Peter, the leader of the apostles, to take that role.

After he rose from the dead, Jesus could not just live forever on this earth. If he remained on earth his enemies would have kept on trying to kill him. If he just disappeared, people would assume that he had wandered off to die someplace quietly. If he faded away or vanished from their sight they would conclude that Jesus hadn't risen from the dead physically, but that they had simply seen a ghost.

Jesus had to go away, but to make it clear that he had really physically risen from the dead, and that he was not going to die again, he had to go to the spiritual realm in a visibly physical way. Jesus therefore made sure that his followers saw him physically depart from this earth.

Forty days after he rose from the dead he took his apostles to a hill outside Jerusalem. He gave them his own authority and power told them to continue his work. To confirm his promise Jesus said his Spirit would help them to do his work in the world. Then he rose up, and they watched him go from their sight.

Is it difficult to believe that Jesus rose up from earth to heaven? If you accept that Jesus is who he says he is (God in human form) then it makes sense that he would not be able to stay dead. It also follows that once he had risen from the dead, he would need to go away in a physical manner.

Having Jesus disappear into a cloud sounds like a fantasy story, but how else could it have happened? We know that heaven is not a big golden city on the other side of the clouds. Heaven is a spiritual realm. But because Jesus had to be seen to move physically to the spiritual realm, the spiritual realm had to be located somewhere, and the sky is the best symbol we have for the spiritual realm.

However, Jesus didn't leave this earth for heaven simply to tie up the loose ends of the story. His return to heaven was also the completion of his destiny. By going to heaven as a human being he opened up the way for us to follow. By returning to heaven he took his place in that realm as the victorious hero returning home.

The Fire and Wind Come Down

After Jesus went to the spiritual realm his followers waited in Jerusalem. The Bible says they prayed and worshipped together along with Mary, the mother of Jesus and others who had witnessed the resurrection. The apostles were the ones Jesus had specially chosen, and Peter was their leader, just as Christ had requested. While they waited for the gift Jesus had promised, the apostles remembered Jesus through the simple memorial meal as he had commanded them. When he had celebrated the ancient Jewish Passover feast with them just before his death, Jesus had said the bread was his body and the wine was his blood. The apostles believed that, in a miraculous way beyond human understanding, the bread and wine at this meal really did become the body and blood of Christ. In this way Jesus was present with them just as he promised he would be. As they ate the bread and drank the wine that had become the body and blood of Christ they became part of Jesus and he became a part of them.

At this time—just over forty days after the Passover festival—the apostles, along with Jews from all around the world had gathered in Jerusalem for another Jewish festival called Pentecost. Pentecost marked the end of the Passover season and the beginning of the harvest season. Pentecost was also a celebration of God's revelation (the Ten Commandments) to Moses on Mount Sinai. At Sinai God's presence was manifested in an earthquake, wind, and fire.

As a fulfillment of this event the apostles also experienced a powerful manifestation of God's presence. Suddenly as they were together there was the sound of a mighty wind and they saw flames of fire appear over the heads of the apostles and their followers.

The little group of Jesus' followers felt a surge of power within them. This experience must have been overwhelming, because it is recorded that they were reeling and falling over with the effects of this sudden supernatural spiritual experience—so much so that the observers joked that they were drunk.

Then Peter stood up and got everyone's attention. He said his friends weren't drunk, as it was only nine o'clock in the morning. Instead, they were filled with the Holy Spirit just as Jesus had promised.

Powerful Preaching

On that day Peter preached with amazing power and insight. Before these events he had been cowardly and confused. Now he was a powerful leader. The power Jesus had promised had come upon him. Peter told the Jewish people gathered there about Jesus, who had been killed, but had risen again. He reminded them that many people had seen Jesus alive, and that Jesus had risen again because it was simply impossible for death to hold him. He quoted passages from the Jewish religious writings to show the Jews how Jesus had fulfilled their ancient prophecies. Then he declared that the resurrection proved that Jesus was exactly who he said he was: the Jewish Messiah; the anointed servant of God; the very Son of God.

Then Peter delivered the final thrust. He told the Jewish leaders that they had crucified their own Messiah. Many people were swayed by Peter's powerful preaching and asked what they had to do. He answered, "Repent and be baptized in the name of Jesus Christ for the forgiveness of sins and you will receive the gift of the Holy Spirit."

At that moment the essence of the Christian religion became clear. Human beings may have killed the one who was sent to save them, but in doing so, he accomplished what he was sent for. Human evil may have been great, but God's love was greater. By allowing himself to be a victim of evil, Jesus Christ defeated evil and death forever, and was able to offer a share in his victory to all people.

Peter said that we are able to join ourselves with Christ's victory in three simple steps. First we have to realize that, even though part of us wants to do good, all of us have chosen the selfish way in life. We have hurt ourselves and other. If we had been there in Jerusalem that fateful week we probably would have consented to Jesus' death, or at least stood silent and done nothing about it. Once we realize that we are on the side of evil, we must be sorry for the fact.

The second step is to switch sides. We must decide to live life God's way, not our way. Furthermore, we must accept that it is through Jesus' death and resurrection that we have the power to make this decision and stick with it.

As a sign of our decision, we must be plunged into water while invoking God the Father, Jesus his Son, and the Holy Spirit. By this physical action our inner decision to change is put into action. By this process we are washed clean spiritually and enter into Jesus' life. The wrong things we have done are forgiven, and we receive the Spirit that Jesus had promised. Through this threefold action the New Testament says we are "born again" and given a fresh start in life as members of God's family.

Anyone can begin this process at any time. If you have understood this simple core of the Christian faith now, as you read this, then you can take the first two steps—being sorry and switching sides—right now. All it takes is for you to speak to God, saying that you are sorry, that you believe Jesus Christ died and rose again for your sake, and that you want to change your life. If you have already been baptized, then by making this decision you have begun to claim what was done for you in baptism. If you have not been baptized, then you need to search out your local Catholic Church and talk to a priest, who will help you take the next step.

Twelve Timid Men

Did the events of Pentecost really happen? After all, there have been similar stories of mighty winds, supernatural flames, and people speaking in strange heavenly languages right down to the present day. These supernatural, religious events are not the best evidence that something amazing occurred in Jerusalem that day.

Something stupendous must have happened because of the historical and human results. Before Pentecost Peter was a coward. The night Jesus was arrested and taken away, Peter had denied that he even knew Jesus. The other apostles weren't much better. They were confused, frightened, ordinary men who were unsure of themselves and unsure who Jesus really was.

What happened to transform these twelve timid men into religious leaders who spearheaded a movement that eventually challenged the Roman Empire and transformed human history? Peter was ready to run away, but in the end he led the first Christians to stand up courageously for the truth, and later died for his faith as a martyr. What happened to turn Peter from a weak coward to a powerful and fearless world leader who would eventually go to Rome and lay down his life for his beliefs?

The resurrection and ascension of Jesus released the power that came down at Pentecost. The three events are dependent on each other. The same power that raised Jesus from the dead was suddenly available to transform ordinary people's lives. Ever since that momentous day in Jerusalem, the experiences of other Christians have proved that weak, ordinary people really can be transformed by this resurrection force.

Peter's is just one example of a life transformed. There are countless others. Francis of Assisi was a confused young soldier home from the wars, but he was converted from a spoiled dreamer of a rich boy into the founder of a powerful religious order that changed the world.

Mother Teresa was just an ordinary nun teaching in a convent school, but the same power that transformed Peter and Francis of Assisi turned her into a spiritual dynamo who established an international movement. She went on to challenge presidents and prime ministers with her message of the preciousness of human life. Karol Wojtyla was an ordinary young student, but God's power transformed him into Pope John Paul the Great—a man who changed the course of history.

The conversion experiences described in the New Testament are echoed in millions of ordinary lives down through history. The evidence of transformed lives is everywhere, and if it happened to Peter and Francis of Assisi and Mother Teresa and Pope John Paul, then it can happen to you and to me too.

A Global Vision

This is how Jesus planned to transform the whole world: by transforming individuals who would change the world. He said that a seed could not grow unless it first falls into the ground and dies. He also said that his kingdom was like a tiny seed that is planted, then grows into a huge tree, full of life and power.

Jesus was the little seed that died and was buried. His resurrection was the growth and blossoming of that great tree. The gift of the Holy Spirit is like the life-giving sap in that tree. The whole family of Christ's followers down through the ages is like the tree that is growing to provide a place of shelter and shade for the whole world.

At Pentecost God's plan for the renewal and trans-formation of the world became clear. By his death and resurrection, Jesus Christ released a power into the world that would continue to work through the world, as current surges through an electrical system. This force is always there working to bring about new life;

to rescue all that is soiled and dying, and bring it to a fresh, new beginning. Furthermore, the same creative Spirit that was released at Pentecost had been active from the beginning of time.

Chapter Two

The Transformer

The Spirit of Creation

At Pentecost humanity experienced the spiritual equivalent of a huge volcano. Forces that had been bubbling beneath the surface suddenly burst out with enormous power. Before Pentecost God's Spirit had been surging and working in the world, but in a more general way. When Jesus came, the work of the Spirit came into focus. When he died and rose again Jesus released God's powerful Spirit into the world in a more specific way.

Because the Holy Spirit was at work in the world from the beginning it is worth looking to the past to see how and what he did. By seeing how the Holy Spirit worked in the Old Testament we can then can understand how the Spirit is focused in the life and teaching of Jesus Christ. Seeing this will then help us to understand how the Spirit can transform our lives today.

At the beginning of the Bible the Jewish people recorded their ancient creation story. They were not giving a scientific and historical account of the beginning of the world. Instead, in simple, poetic language they described how God was the source of all things from the beginning. In majestic words they said, "In the beginning God created the heavens and the earth and the earth was without form. It was empty, and the breath of God moved over the surface of the deep watery chaos."

Two pictures come together in these ancient words. One is the image of a great bird hovering over the watery chaos. That shadowy presence was there from the beginning as the creative power behind all things. The other image is of "God's breath." By breathing over the watery darkness God brought life into existence.

This "hovering spirit" or "breath of God" can also be understood as the "Spirit of God." In other words, God's Holy Spirit was there at the beginning, as the creative force in the world. Later in the creation story the same spirit brings man to life because God "breathes into Adam the breath of life."

Jesus and the Creator Spirit

At creation the Holy Spirit, like a great hovering bird, brought new life out of the waters of chaos. The same image was echoed at the baptism of Jesus. When he came up out of the water he saw the Spirit like a dove hovering over him. The symbolism is the same:

the Spirit of God is present to bring forth a new kind of spiritual life.

As the "breath of God" brought creation into being, and breathed life into the first human, so after his resurrection Jesus breathed on his apostles and said, "receive the Holy Spirit." This is a symbol that they were being re-created, and that humanity was getting a fresh start with a new breath of God.

It is no coincidence that at Pentecost the followers of Jesus heard the sound of a mighty rushing wind. The creative breath that Jesus had blown on his apostles in a symbolic way was the same breath of God that had blown over the world at the beginning of creation. The same Spirit of new life is now available to breathe new life into our stale, confused existence. The Spirit that brought creation out of chaos is actively seeking to create order out of the chaos and confusion of our lives.

The Spirit of Liberty

The Spirit's character is revealed by what the Spirit does. In the Old Testament one of the things God does is liberate from slavery and death. The story of Exodus reveals how God saved the Jewish people from death and brought them into freedom from their slavery in Egypt.

Moses was a young Jewish man who had been brought up in the court of the Egyptian pharaoh. After committing a murder he had to flee for his life into the wilderness. In the desert he married and settled down to live as a nomadic shepherd.

Then one day as he was tending his sheep Moses was startled by a vision of a bush on fire. When he looked closer he saw that although the bush was burning it was not being consumed by the flames.

Moses heard a voice that seemed to come from within the bush. The voice said that it was the God of his Jewish ancestors, and that Moses was destined to return to Egypt to lead the Jews out of slavery to freedom in their own land.

Eventually Moses obeyed. In Egypt the Spirit delivered the Jewish people from terrible plagues and a sure death. When they were finally released the Jewish people were led on their journeys by a cloud that was like a pillar of fire. The burning bush and the cloudy pillar of fire were powerful symbols of the Holy Spirit. The fire brought light and warmth and led them into freedom.

Jesus and the Fire of Freedom

John the Baptist's message was also about freedom from slavery and death. He announced that someone greater than himself would soon appear. John said, "I have baptized with water, but one is coming who will baptize you with the Holy Spirit and with fire." Then Jesus appeared and was baptized by John.

Straight after his baptism Jesus went out into the desert where he went through a time of spiritual testing. Then he went to his hometown of Nazareth and announced his mission. He went into the synagogue (which was the local Jewish church) and read a passage from the Old Testament prophet Isaiah which said, "The Spirit of the Lord is upon me, because he has anointed me to preach good news to the poor. He has sent me to proclaim release to the captives and recovery of sight to the blind, to set at liberty those who are oppressed."

Everyone stared at him. What could he mean? The passage Jesus had read referred to the expected servant of God, the anointed one—the Messiah. Then to their amazement Jesus said with complete confidence, "Today this prophecy is fulfilled in your hearing." Just as the Holy Spirit had led the Jews out of slavery, Jesus claimed to have a special calling to do the same thing.

Jesus' ministry was only the start. When the tongues of fire appeared on the day of Pentecost, God was using the same symbol of fire to show that the Spirit who had liberated the Jewish people from slavery in Egypt was now given to deliver people from slavery to their twisted selfish nature.

Each one of us is enslaved to some sort of selfishness or weakness. The fiery energy force that delivered the Jewish people is now available to us. The Holy Spirit can deliver us from the slavery of our addictions; he can liberate us from our fears and our selfishness and lead us to a new spiritual life—a life that is abundant and free.

The Spirit of Wisdom

The Jewish people finally came into their Promised Land, and eventually a king was chosen to rule over them. King David consolidated the kingdom and established peace and prosperity. He was succeeded by his son Solomon.

During this time the different civilizations around Israel had started to write down their wise sayings—"quotable quotes" that helped people to cope with life's challenges. The Jewish people, too, developed their own forms of "wisdom literature." They added drama, poetry, and stories to the quotable quotes to have memorable ways of passing their wisdom from one generation to the next. Solomon was considered the wisest king of the time because he was a master of this kind of practical wisdom.

Eventually the Jewish people came to understand that wisdom was not only practical advice for dealing with life's problems. If a person really wanted to be wise he would have to ask the big questions about life: Why are we here? Is there a God? Why must we die? How can God be good yet allow suffering?

The Jews realized that people couldn't answer these questions on their own. The big questions are so difficult to answer, and there was so much disagreement, that the Jews realized they needed to have the truth revealed to them by a higher power. They visualized a "Spirit of Wisdom" that led them to enlightenment and spiritual understanding.

Wisdom and Wave Walking

The Gospel of Luke tells us on two occasions that as a boy Jesus "grew in wisdom." Luke doesn't simply mean that Jesus was getting a good education. Luke understood from the Old Testament that "wisdom" was another name for the Holy Spirit.

Jesus' connection to God's holy wisdom, or Spirit, continues throughout the gospels. For example, the Jews thought of the sea as a dangerous and chaotic place. In some Old Testament passages God is the one who calms the sea and walks on the waves, and in one of the Old Testament wisdom poems it is Wisdom who "walks on the waves of the sea."

In the gospels Jesus calms a storm and in one story he comes to his followers by walking across the waves. These stories were not told simply to impress people with Jesus' ability to do miracles. The gospel writers told the stories to make people consider who Jesus really was—the one in whom the Spirit of Wisdom lived.

The people who first heard these stories knew who had the power to calm the storm and walk on the waves. So when Jesus performed these powerful actions his followers rightly asked the question, "Who is this man?"

They knew from the Old Testament that "God is the one who brings creation out of watery chaos. God is the one who calms the storm, and it is the Holy Spirit of Wisdom who walks on the waves of the sea." Since Jesus calmed the storm and walked on the waves, the first Christians concluded that Jesus was the Wisdom of God in human form.

When Jesus sent his Spirit onto individuals at Pentecost they realized that the same Spirit of Wisdom who had led the ancient Jews to understand the Truth was also with them to lead and guide them into all truth. That same Spirit of Wisdom is available to each one of us. All we need to do is ask.

Tapping into the Power

Throughout the history of the Jewish people the Spirit of creation continued to bring them into new life. The same Spirit continued to lead them into freedom whenever they fell back into the slavery of selfish, destructive behavior. Through their poets, priests, and preachers the Spirit continued to teach them and bring them to new insights and understandings about themselves and God.

By the work of the Spirit the Jews were being prepared for the coming of Jesus, and through their history, God would open up the whole world to a fresh understanding of his goodness and truth. When Jesus came he did the same things in a specific way that the Holy Spirit had done within the history of the Jewish people.

Jesus brought new life. He said, "I have come that you may have life in all its fullness." Jesus also brought freedom. By healing people he delivered them from the bondage of ill health. By forgiving their sins he delivered them from guilt, fear, and darkness. Jesus also taught them the truth about God, and so led them in the paths of real wisdom.

But Jesus was not just full of the Holy Spirit, as another religious leader might be. He was actually *one* with the Holy Spirit. Likewise, Jesus did not simply teach people about God the Father. He said, "I and the Father are one."

In other words, Jesus is the connecting point between God the Father and the Holy Spirit. He is also the junction point between us and God. This unity between Jesus, the Holy Spirit, and the Father is vital because it shows us where we can get the power needed for our lives to be transformed.

Jesus does not just teach us about God and the Holy Spirit. He takes us into real, powerful contact with God. In order to understand how this happens we have to understand better how Jesus, the Father, and the Holy Spirit live and work as one.

Dwight Longenecker

Chapter Three
Father, Son and Holy Spirit

Why the Holy Trinity?

Probably the most unusual and difficult belief that
Christians hold is the idea that the one God is a *Trinity*
of three persons: Father, Son, and Holy Spirit. It makes
sense to many people that there is only one God. They
quite rightly say that God is a total and utter mystery,
ultimately beyond our powers of understanding or
description. They wonder why we have to bother with
such a difficult and seemingly contradictory idea as
the Trinity.

One of the reasons we bother is because, as the first
Christians began to think about the way God worked in
the world, they came to realize that Jesus acted like God
in human form. They realized that Jesus did the things
that, in the Old Testament, God's Holy Spirit had done.
It was by thinking about Jesus that they came to understand that he was one with the Spirit and the Father.

The resulting concept is difficult to understand intellectually, but if we try to put ourselves into the shoes of the first Christians we will see that this explanation about God's character fits best with the other things we know about God.

Despite the difficulties, the Trinity is the best way of understanding God. Furthermore, this understanding is not just a head game. This truth about God is practical. It really does help the other pieces of the puzzle fit into place. Understanding more of the Holy Trinity helps us to understand God better. More importantly, it helps us experience God better.

God Talk

Since God is ultimately beyond our comprehension it is appropriate to use a mysterious concept to indicate what he is like. The Trinity itself is a mystery—that is to say, it is a truth we can experience, even if we cannot fully explain it. That might sound a little suspicious, but when you think about it there is another, very ordinary aspect of life where this is also true. Love is something we can experience, but which we cannot fully explain. The Trinity is like that too.

The mystery of the Trinity has been explained with many different types of picture language. Saint Patrick said it was like clover leaf—one leaf, but three leaves. Others have said it is like water—it takes three different forms—solid, liquid, and gas, but all three are still water. All of these descriptions might help people understand the Trinity, but none of them are totally satisfactory. They can never be more than picture language to try to explain what is beyond our ability to understand.

One of the reasons none of these word pictures works completely is because all of them are just pictures. If God is Three in One, then we can't make a picture of him. This is because God the Three in One is as much about what God does as what he is.

We call the Father, Son and Holy Spirit "persons" because like any person, they have three ways of acting. While saying that, it is also true that where one person of the Trinity acts all three are also acting. You could say all three act together in three different ways.

The Family God

That is why the best way to speak of the Holy Trinity is to talk about family life. God's life is not empty and dead. Instead it is a dynamic loving relationship among three persons. The Father, the Son, and the Holy Spirit are like a human family. A man, woman, and child are united as one through the love in a marriage, and that three-way union of love reflects the nature of God himself.

If God is like a family, then at the core of God's life is love. This is the practical and beautiful truth that is unlocked by the mystery of the Holy Trinity: that God is Love. If God is love, then we come to know God by learning more about love. We also experience the reality of the Trinity by experiencing the reality of God's love in our lives.

We learn best about love by being members of a family. That is why when we become Christians it is said that we are being "adopted" as God's children. This not only means that we enter the family of all other people who believe, but we enter the "family" that is made up of Father, Son, and Holy Spirit.

Welcome Home

This is what Jesus came to accomplish. He broke down the barrier between God and humanity in order to welcome us into a relationship with his own father God. Like an older brother, Jesus came into this world to seek and to save his lost brothers and sisters and bring them home.

We claim our family inheritance by realizing we are cut off from God, deciding to switch sides, and being baptized. Baptism is a ritual that brings about the truth it signifies. Being put into the water at baptism is a sign of being put into Christ's death. Rising up out of the water is a sign of rising up with Christ in his resurrection. In other words, through baptism we are "put into" Christ. We become one with Christ and he becomes one with us.

When Jesus was baptized the voice from heaven said, "This is my beloved son" and the Holy Spirit descended like a dove. This was a picture that in baptism Father, Son, and Holy Spirit are together as one, powerful, dynamic unit.

Therefore, when you become a Christian you are baptized not just in the name of Christ, but in the name of the Father, the Son, and the Holy Spirit. This is because through baptism we enter into a relationship with the God who is Father, Son, and Holy Spirit.

Just as the Father said to Jesus, "You are my beloved Son," so at our baptism into Jesus Christ God says to us, "You are my beloved child." Through this transaction we become part of God's family. God becomes our Father. Jesus becomes our Brother and the Holy Spirit enters our life to bring us right into the center of that reality that is God himself.

Christ's Life Within Us

If you have stayed with me thus far you will see that the Christian faith is not simply about obeying a set of religious rules or just trying hard to be a good person. Christianity is far more radical than that. The Christian faith is about accepting God into the very core of our lives. When we are baptized, the life force that raised Jesus Christ from the dead enters our life and begins a process of transformation within us.

Father, Son, and Holy Spirit exist in perfect unity. As Christ enters into our life he wants to create a new unity with us. Jesus prayed that his followers might be one as he and the Father are one. Jesus was "one" with the Father in what he was—like the Father, fully divine—but also in what he *did*. That's the oneness that we are to imitate. All the chaotic, divided parts of us are to be harmonized and work together in unity. Our body, our mind, and our spirit are meant to work as one—not be divided against each other. Likewise we should work in harmony with other people, united in a common purpose of truth and love.

It is important to get a small glimpse of what the Holy Trinity means, because then we come to realize the simple truth that as we accept Christ into our lives we are opening the very heart of our being to God himself. The three way God of Love is working in and through us to bring us to our final destiny. That destiny is nothing less than a life lived within the everlasting power and glory of God's own life of love.

Love binds them all together

Just as it is impossible to fully explain love, it is impossible to fully explain the Trinity (though wise theologians over the centuries have certainly helped advance our understanding). But just as it is possible to know love by experiencing it, so it is possible to begin to understand the Trinity by experiencing God's powerful love.

By "love" I don't mean the sentimental stuff of romantic movies and love songs. These are fine, but I am talking about something far greater, and far more mysterious and noble and tragic and true. The love I am talking about really is the "force" that binds all things together.

The force that moves the sun and the other stars is the power of Love. Love is the outgoing, goodness of God in the universe. Love is also the power that binds the three persons of the Trinity together. Love attracts the Father, the Son, and the Holy Spirit and binds them in a perfect harmony and unity like a great magnetic force. This is the powerful love that we are called to share in. Love binds us together with one another, but it also binds us into the very heart of the Trinity. We tap into that love and become a part of it as you might plug into an electric circuit.

All You Need Is Love

To be a Christian therefore means learning to live and move within and through the power of Love. The New Testament says, "Those who live in love live in God and God lives in them." As we live a life of love for ourselves, for our families, for other people, and for the world we are not just making the world a better, nicer place, but we are also joining ourselves with the heart of God.

The love of God is the energy force that draws us into relationship with him, but all of our lesser loves on earth are also part of that greater love. When we live in the love of a human family, when we engage in loving actions towards others, when we forgive and make time for others, we do so within the greater love that binds God together, and which moves the sun and the stars.

Jesus Christ is the way for us to be bound into this wonderful energy supply called love. He shows us that love in its fullness and empowers us to live within that love more and more each day. Do you want to have a full and abundant life and make the world a better place? Do you want to find true love in this life, and a love that will last forever? Do you want to discover the secret of true happiness? Do you want to live life to the full and take hold of all that life has to offer?

Then open your life to this power of Love. It is available to all. It is not easy to claim it, for everything within us whispers that we should turn away from this Love. But if we give ourselves to this love and ask for the gift of this love, then it will most certainly be given and we will be able to begin the greatest adventure that life has to offer.

Down through the ages real, ordinary people have been transformed by the power of God's love in their lives. They have given themselves totally to this love and it has burned in their lives with such radiance and power that the whole world has seen their lives transformed. How this amazing transformation can happen is the subject of the next section.

Chapter Four

Going with God

Connecting with the Power Source

For some time I have been talking about the power of transformation in our lives, and where that power comes from. I've done this because it is important to realize that we cannot change ourselves. Bookstores are full of self-help books. These contain much that is good and helpful, but there is a basic flaw in all of them. They don't put you in touch with a power greater than yourself.

Christians believe that God's Holy Spirit gives us an amazing power source for change in our lives. Because of Jesus Christ's death and resurrection that power source is available to every person who asks for it. This burning energy source is necessary if we really want to change for good.

It's not hard to connect with this fire force, but the first and most important step is to realize that we need this power of change in our lives, and that we cannot change on our own.

Turning Around

One reason self-help books sell so well is that we all want to believe that we can change without the help of God. I'm sorry. We can't. We just don't have the power to change permanently on our own. Of course we can make improvements to our lives, but we cannot change the way we really are deep down inside.

There is only one power that can bring that kind of inner transformation, and that it the spiritual power unleashed by the Holy Spirit. The first step to receiving this power is to realize that we need it. This means we have to change our mind. We have to see, first of all, that we cannot change ourselves by ourselves. This means we have to experience a very fundamental shift in our attitude.

We do not need just an ordinary type of changed mind. Instead we need a radical realignment of our whole life. We need to see that we are headed in the wrong direction and resolve to change course entirely.

Realizing that we are on the wrong course is not the same thing as saying we are totally and utterly wrong in everything. It just means we have been building on sand when we should have been building on solid rock. It means we begin to say, "I need help."

Come Down O Love Divine

Really admitting that we need help doesn't come easily. The conviction that we really are all right as we are dies hard. Sometimes we only come to a true reversal of our attitude because we have reached rock bottom in life. Through illness, bereavement, bad luck, or our own stupid choices we come to the point where we have nowhere else to turn, and we realize then at the very deepest level of our personalities that we need help and only God can bail us out.

This ground level change of heart is not just admitting that in theory we need help, but *knowing* that we need help. Then we can really turn to God and ask for the Holy Spirit to come to our aid. At that point we are open to receive the gift of Divine Love or the gift of the Holy Spirit in a new way.

If we are not at rock bottom, but we still want to understand what this kind of change of heart is about, then it is enough to ask for the gift of "repentance." Repentance is a technical word for this ground-level shift of awareness. When we ask for the gift of repentance we will begin to understand our deepest need in a more powerful way. Then, once we have realized our need, we are ready to receive the power to change.

Jesus Christ released that power in the world. All we need to do is acknowledge that fact and ask for his Spirit within our lives. He has promised to send that Spirit, and if we ask we will most certainly receive. If we seek, he has promised that we will find the treasure. Trusting that he will give us the power to change is called "faith."

Teamwork Required

Having repentance and faith is not a once-and-done thing. It is true that we need to come to a set time when we really do turn towards God, but we also need to check our spiritual compass daily. Day by day, throughout our lives, we need to check whether we are aware of our need for God and if we are living in faith.

Living this way is an adventure. It means new possibilities open up, because God is in charge now, not us. Those who live by faith are on a journey into a new and unknown land—a land that promises to be full of new riches as well as new challenges.

Living in repentance and faith opens us up to God's marvelous way of working in the world. Suddenly we can see that someone else is working in and through our lives to transform us into all that we can be. Furthermore, he is working through us to change the world. We realize that we have become his agents in the world, and that if we stay with him fantastic and wonderful things can happen.

To stay in this state of repentance and faith we must work with the Holy Spirit. The help that God gives us, first to understand him and then to turn towards him regularly, is called "grace." Living in a "state of grace" means that we dwell constantly in an awareness that we need God, and that he is always by our side.

The Great Challenge

God helps us to see our need and to turn towards him, but we must always remember that God will not override our will. He will not force us to love him. If he did, the result would not be love. For love to be real we must choose to turn from our own way and follow God's way.

God gives us the power to choose, and the specific power to choose him and his love, but we must use that power to be transformed into all God created us to be

The work of total transformation is not easy or quick. In fact you will find that trying to follow God's way is the hardest thing you have ever done. Those of us who are trying to follow this path admit that we often get confused and lose our way. Many times we stumble and fall on the path to perfection. What matters is not how often we fall, but how often we get up.

The sign that the Holy Spirit is at work in our lives is that we can see new powers developing. A new order grows within us; certain abilities that were lying dormant suddenly start to develop; in many practical ways our lives begin to change. The Spirit gives these new powers to help us to grow as people and to better understand God's ways and wisdom.

The Gifts of the Holy Spirit

The gifts of the Holy Spirit are supernatural gifts. They are qualities of mind, intelligence, and spirit that help us to grow into all that God created us to be. Although they are supernatural gifts, they are expressed and worked out in our lives in seemingly natural ways.

The Holy Spirit gives a whole range of different new abilities, but there are seven recognized gifts that we can notice becoming active in people's lives. The first of the seven gifts of the Holy Spirit is wisdom. Wisdom was the power of God that helped to make all things. Wisdom helps us to see clearly; to get our priorities right and grow in understanding.

Understanding is the second gift of the Holy Spirit. It is not easy to understand spiritual matters. Our eyes are darkened by sin, but the Holy Spirit has been given to teach us all things. As we learn more about our faith the Holy Spirit is there as our teacher and mentor. With the gift of understanding, our range of interests changes. We discover that we are more interested in spiritual matters.

It is difficult to know the right way through life. We are often faced with difficult decisions. As we learn to listen to the Holy Spirit in our lives these decisions become easier. We are able to see the right way and discern what is best. The ability to discern what is right and wrong and understand which spiritual things are true and false is called "counsel" and is the third gift of the Spirit.

The fourth gift is "fortitude." This is the supernatural strength to do what is right. When we are faced with a temptation, if we ask the Holy Spirit for help it will be there. In practical terms "fortitude" helps us to stand up for what is right.

Knowledge is another gift of the Holy Spirit. This is not just head knowledge, but a real experience of spiritual truths. This kind of knowledge of life is the kind you have when you're in love, not the kind you get from reading love poems. The spiritual gift of knowledge is not purely intellectual. It is practical and useful. With this kind of knowledge we can help others to know the truth and live by it.

"Piety" is the gift to live the spiritual life in all naturalness and goodness. It is not about trying hard to be holy and good, but the supernatural ability to be holy and good with joy and ease. A truly "pious" person does try hard to be good, but eventually the Spirit brings him to a place where he does good as part of his nature. This is like an athlete who trains hard, but then wins the race with ease and a sense of exhilaration.

The last gift is "fear of the Lord." This does not mean that we tremble in constant anxiety in the face of God. Instead it means that we live in a state of repentance and faith. "Fear of the Lord" is a constant awareness that we need God and that he is with us always.

Chapter Five
Total Transformation

Signs of Life

When the Holy Spirit begins to work in our life, it is as if we become a new person. The old things have passed away, and all things have become new. Not only do we see ourselves in a new away, but we see everyone else in a new light too. Indeed, we see the whole world in a new way.

As we live in the Spirit, other people will begin to see that there is something different about us. Perhaps they can't define it, but they realize that our priorities have changed. The Holy Spirit has given us a new way of seeing, and a new way of being.

Of course the new person is not made perfect immediately. We have to work hard with God for the Holy Spirit to really take control of our lives. But eventually we find that our old habits are replaced by new ways of thinking and behaving. Bit by bit in our daily lives we find that real change is taking place. We really *are* becoming more patient with our children, our difficult family members, or that difficult person at work.

The Spirit works within our ordinary lives to give them an extraordinary wealth of meaning, purpose, and power. This process of perfection is gradual and natural. Like the growth of a great tree, it takes time for the roots to go deep. It takes time for the branches to grow and for the fruit to ripen, but when the fruit is ripe everyone benefits.

Likewise, the Spirit brings to fruition certain recognizable traits within the spiritual person. These characteristics are called the fruit of the Holy Spirit. The fruits of the Holy Spirit are developed by the supernatural work of the Spirit. Although the Spirit is supernatural, his work is not un-natural. The fruits of the Spirit are the best of our human character brought to full development by the Spirit's power.

The Fruits of Life

The first fruit is "charity." Charity is not just giving money to an organization that helps poor people. Neither is charity simply doing good to others. Instead it is an inner quality; the perfection of love in which we see and love others as they are. In our daily lives "charity" means we become naturally more patient and tolerant because deep down we really have come to desire the best for others—not just for ourselves.

Joy is the second fruit that the Spirit helps to ripen

in our lives. Joy is not just happiness or fun. Instead Christian joy is a supernatural kind of happiness. Joy is marked by a special spiritual energy and enthusiasm for life. The Spirit brings joy because the person can see that an all-loving God is at work in the world. Because of this they can genuinely see the positive side of every problem.

Joy is linked with the third fruit: peace. The Bible talks about "the peace that passes all understanding" and Jesus said to his disciples, "I give you peace. Not peace as the world gives." The person who lives in the power of the Holy Spirit knows a deep peace despite things going wrong. The Spirit-filled person has peace because he knows that God is in charge, and in the end all shall be well.

Along with inner peace and charity comes patience and kindness. For a Christian patience and kindness are not simply a matter of being polite and having good manners. Instead the person who is filled with the Holy Spirit is patient and kind not because he's trying to be, but because genuine patience and kindness have become part of his nature.

It is the same thing with the other fruits of the Spirit. A person is good, generous, gentle, faithful, and modest not so much because he is trying hard to be that way, but because his nature has been transformed, and he has become all that God created him to be.

Becoming Sons and Daughters of God

This is the exciting destiny for all people. We really are created to be the sons and daughters of God—brothers and sisters of Christ. Over and over again throughout the writings of the New Testament, and in the lives of Christian saints we hear the call not to live a life of rules and regulations, but a life that is transformed by the power of God.

Religion has become irrelevant and meaningless to many people because of this fundamental mistake. They have misunderstood the most important thing. Jesus did not come to enforce a long list of rules. The Christian faith is not first and foremost, a religion of respectability and good manners. It is a religion that transforms, and glorifies individual human beings.

This is not easy, but Therese of Lisieux calls us to the challenge with youthful zeal, "You cannot be half a saint," she cries, "you must be a whole saint, or no saint at all!" A saint is not simply a pious, goody-goody type of person. The saints are brave, idealistic, unyielding and totally devoted heroes. They are the spiritual equivalents of world champion mountain climbers. The saints are utterly committed to their beliefs. They loved God with all the heart, mind, and strength.

In doing so, they show us the possibility of total transformation into radiant and powerful people. This is what Christianity is about, no less than the total transformation of our lives into all that we were created to be—and what we are created to be—and what we are created to be is eternal being—sons and daughters of the living God.

Change the World (and Start with Yourself)

Not only are we called to be totally converted ourselves, but as this action takes place in our lives, it is also happening in the lives of millions of other people all over the world. The work of the Holy Spirit down through the ages is to convert not just individuals to the will of God, but to bring the whole world back into relationship with him.

Do you want to change the world? Change yourself first, by opening yourself up to the power of the Person who made you. As the Holy Spirit transforms our lives we begin to fit into God's plan for the whole world. We become part of a worldwide movement that is changing the course of history.

The study of history shows that it is the religious ideas of individuals and nations that motivate the transformation of history. Believers transform the world. Unbelievers cannot even transform themselves. As we believe, so we will do, and if we believe then the Holy Spirit will transform our lives so we can be part of his action in the world.

There is a group of people in the world who will have given themselves to have this very action. This international group of believers are all empowered by the Holy Spirit. All of them are all working together with the spirit as much as they can. Before Jesus left

this earth he not only gave his Holy Spirit to his followers, but he also told his followers to form a community of all those who were filled with his Holy
Spirit. This little group of Holy Spirit people has grown
for the last 2,000 years, filling every corner of the
world. This group of people is called the Church.

Chapter Six
The People of God

As It Was in the Beginning

From the very beginning God began his work on earth within a family. The Jewish writers were keen to show that they had descended from their father Abraham, and that he had descended from Adam and Eve. In other words, the special relationship that God established with Adam and Eve continued down through the generations.

The Old Testament is the story not just of Spirit-filled individuals like Abraham, Moses, Joshua, David and the prophets. It is also the story of a Spirit-filled people we call the Jews. Throughout the Old Testament God is concerned with the whole family of Abraham—not just with certain individuals.

This shows God's way of working in the world. He works through a chosen group of people. God's Spirit fills the individuals in that family, but the Spirit also directs the whole people of God. God works in the world both through individuals and through a whole body of faithful people.

The Church is the Family of Christ

The same Holy Spirit that filled, renewed, guided, and taught the Old Testament people of God was given to the followers of Jesus at Pentecost. In this a new kind of spiritual family was established. Because each individual has a share in the same spirit there is a family bond between them. Jesus said that each one is his brother or sister. He said, "the one who does the will of my father is my brother or my sister."

If those who receive the Holy Spirit are brothers and sisters of Jesus, then they are also brothers and sisters of each other. Because they share in the same spirit they are members of the same family. This is not just or a symbol or a way of speaking. This is a reality. Through the Holy Spirit every other Christian is my spiritual brother or sister.

The Church, therefore, is not simply a collection of like-minded people. A political party, a sports team, an academic society—all of these are simply organizations of people with certain shared goals and interests. The Church, on the other hand, is more than that. It is a family. All who belong to it are members of the great family of God.

The Church as the Body of Christ

The Church is a family, but the New Testament uses another image to talk about the people of God. It says that the Church is the "the body of Christ." Each member of the Church is like a cell in the body. As such every member is dependent on every other member. They cannot exist on their own.

Once again, this is not simply a poetic way of speaking. In a very real sense the Church is Christ's body alive here on earth today. The body of all people who believe in Christ do his work in the world.

Those who are alive in the Spirit are alive to one another. The Spirit is constantly at work keeping all the Spirit-filled people working together in harmony like members of a vast orchestra. In this way, all the individual Christians do what they can do best, but at the same time they are working together with one another to accomplish Christ's plan of world transformation.

If the Church is the body of Christ, then we would expect the Church to show Christ at work in the world today. This is exactly what we do find. In earlier chapters we saw how the Spirit brings new life, freedom, and understanding. Then we saw that Jesus did that same work when he was on earth. Now he does this work through the ministry of the Spirit-filled people of God.

The Body of Christ Brings New Life

One of the things the Holy Spirit does is to bring new life. The Holy Spirit was there at the beginning of creation, bringing life out of the dark watery chaos.

Jesus breathed new life into his followers after his resurrection, and he linked this new life with the symbol of water, declaring, "You must be born again of water and the spirit."

I will discuss this more later, but at this point it is enough to say that through the Church we receive the gift of baptism. By cleansing us with water God brings us into a new kind of spiritual life. We receive the gift of the Holy Spirit, but we do so through the ministry of God's people on earth: the Church.

The Church is at work in the world bringing new life in all sorts of ways. Through education, healing ministries, health care, political involvement, pastoral care, and spiritual teaching Christ's body the Church continues to do his work of bringing new life to a dark, dying world.

In our individual lives we find real healing within the family of the Church as well. All of us have dark areas of our lives that need the light of Christ. Whether they are evil things we've done or evil that have been done to us, these wounds can be healed by the power of the Holy Spirit at work in the Church.

If we have committed ourselves to live in the Spirit, then we have our work cut out for us. It is part of our mission first to experience God's healing and wholeness, then to bring that new life to others, so that the whole world can be renewed with God's life.

The Body of Christ Brings Freedom

The Spirit brought freedom. Jesus brought freedom. The Church does the same work. Through forgiveness Jesus set people free to live a new kind of life, and in the Gospels Jesus gave his apostles authority to forgive sins in his name.

Jesus said, "As the Father has sent me so I am sending you." This authority to forgive sins was passed down from the first apostles to the Church leaders who came after them and that same authority can be found in the Church today.

The Spirit, therefore, is not just our private gift. The Spirit should lead each one of us to work with our brothers and sisters to bring freedom, justice, and peace to everyone.

The Church Teaches with Power

In the Old Testament the Holy Spirit taught the people the truth about God. Jesus was the truth about God, and his body on earth (the Church) continues the essential work of teaching people the truth.

When Jesus was on earth the people were amazed because he taught the truth with authority. Before he went back to heaven, Jesus shared with his apostles his authority to know and teach the truth. He said, "All

authority on heaven and on earth has been given to
me, go therefore and teach all nations, baptizing them
in the name of the Father, the Son, and the Holy Spirit.

In other words, Jesus was not only telling his apostles to go out into the world and preach the gospel, he
was also giving them the *authority* to do what he asked
them to do. This would very important. There are
many religious teachers in the world. How would we
know which ones truly speak from God?

Again, I will say more about this later, but it is
enough to say that, through the power of the Holy
Spirit, the Church down through the ages has continued to teach the truth with the same authority of Jesus.
If we want to understand the truth about God most
fully, then we look to Christ, and the Body of Christ
here on earth is the community of Spirit-filled people
that he established.

Not only does the Body of Christ help us to understand the truth about God, but the Spirit that fills the
Church also helps us share that truth with others. If we
are Spirit-filled people, then this is part of our way of
working with the Spirit of Christ in the world.

Getting Ready for the Great Battle

Once we have accepted the Holy Spirit into our
lives we have not reached the end of the journey, we
have only just started. The Christian life is an exciting adventure. It is a difficult pilgrimage to a glorious
destination. Luckily we do not travel alone. In fact, it

is impossible for us to travel this journey alone. By the simple fact that we are all joined to the same body of Christ we are invisibly connected with everyone else who is traveling the same path.

There are many hardships along the way; there are enemies who wish to attack us. We struggle against the dark side of our nature and we struggle against the dark forces arrayed against us.

The next section of this book tells you how to join in the battle. It tells you where to find help. It tells you how God enables you to fight the battle. And it tells you how, through the power of the Holy Spirit, you can fight the good fight, finish the course, and lay hold of the great prize that has been prepared for you.

CATHOLICISM / *Pure and Simple*

Dwight Longenecker

THE GREAT BATTLE

Chapter One
Soldiers of Christ

Conflict Makes the Story

Time and again a favorite story of mine has been voted the best book of the twentieth century. That book is J.R.R. Tolkien's *The Lord of the Rings*.

Not everybody is a fan of fantasy stories, and the adventures of a furry footed hobbit named Frodo simply doesn't interest some people at all. However, the huge popularity of Tolkien's book and the blockbuster success of the films adapted from it indicate that there is something in the story that keeps people coming back for more.

At the very heart of *The Lord of the Rings* and every other classic tale, is the battle of good against evil. You may not be a fan of *The Lord of the Rings*, but whatever kind of story or film you like, some kind conflict likely lies at the heart of the story. The villain may not be supremely evil. Indeed, the thing to be overcome might

161

be the hero's circumstances, disability or personal problem. But whatever it is, there is some evil to be conquered if the good person is going to survive and thrive.

We are captivated by great stories in which the hero fights against evil because deep down we are all aware of some evil in our lives. Evil threatens us from the world around us, but it also threatens us from within. We have a deep instinct that unless we are engaged in the battle against evil we may be consumed by the evil.

Common Sense and the Existence of Evil

Some people think that there's no such thing as good and evil, not *really*. They say that what we call "good" is simply what seems good for us and what we call "evil" is what we think is bad for us. They say that to live together peacefully we need to agree on some basic rights and wrongs; thus "good" and "evil" are just useful terms that help to oil the wheels of society. Can this be so?

It is strange that anyone could hold an opinion like this at the beginning of the twenty-first century. After all, in the last century we have seen some of the most unimaginable evil the world has ever experienced. More people have been unjustly imprisoned, tortured, mutilated, and slaughtered than ever before. Can we face the horrors of Auschwitz, the Rwanda massacres, or the 9/11 attacks and shrug our shoulders and say, "These things only *seemed* evil to the people who died that day"?

This simply won't do. If we have any morsel of humanity within us, then we must conclude that these, and many other examples, are examples of real evil. To fail to call these things evil is not simply to have a different opinion, but to be just plain wrong.

To be honest, we *have* to admit that this evil is at work in the world right now. In fact, one of the reasons this evil has grown is because the people who committed it didn't think it was evil. The Nazis thought the elimination of the Jews was a good and necessary act of ethnic cleansing. The very denial of the reality of good and evil allows the most terrible evils to flourish.

Furthermore, if we are really honest we will admit that there is a shadow side in all of us, that could lead us to commit horrific crimes if the circumstances were right.

We tell ourselves that we would never take part in mass murder, torture of innocent people, or the rape and mutilation of defenseless children. But in the horrors of war and extreme hardship we see that ordinary people do, in fact, both tolerate and commit very terrible crimes—crimes of which they never thought they would be capable.

We Cannot be Neutral

The capability of terrible evil is present in every human heart, and for some it only takes the right circumstances to bring that beast to the surface. Of course, you might want to imagine that the beast is safely chained up in *your* dark places and that you would never do anything terribly wrong. That is what I would like to believe about myself.

I'm not so sure my dark side really is under control. Are you sure yours is under control? When I
lose my temper, when I give into selfish lust or greed
and indulge myself, that beast soon starts showing its
teeth. I start to become less patient and more violent towards those I live with. Furthermore, my own
selfishness not only causes me to do bad things, it also
keeps me from doing good things. The things I want to
do, I can't; and the things I don't want to do, I do.

The fact of the matter is, each one of us is locked
into this battle of good and evil every day of our lives,
whether we like it or not. Because our human nature
is selfish we are in conflict with other people whose
natures are also selfish. Conflict lies at the heart of our
daily existence.

We might wish to opt out of the conflict, but that
is impossible too. If there really is a terrible evil out
there, then, if we are good we must fight against it.
There are only two choices: fight against the evil or
give in to the evil.

Usually the Battle is Clear

It is easy to make this battle more complicated than it
actually is. We can pretend that the battle is difficult to
understand. We can say that "things are never so black
and white" or "it is never clear what is right and wrong."

It's true that some moral choices are difficult and
complicated. But most are not. Most of the time moral
choices are very clear and simple. Living by those

choices may not be easy, but seeing the choice itself is easy. In most situations most people know what is right or wrong. Usually the confusion comes in when people decide they want to do something wrong. Suddenly they imagine that morality is awfully difficult and complex, when all they are really doing is trying to justify their decision to break the rules.

Religion gives us rules to live by, but society does too. The basic rules are universal to all human beings. The details might vary from one society to another, but the essential guidelines can be put quite simply: it is good to live for others and selfish to live only for ourselves. Being untruthful is wrong, telling the truth is right. Hurting others is wrong. Helping others is right. Stealing is wrong. Giving is right. Betraying loved ones is wrong. Being loyal is right.

In most situations, therefore, recognizing the choice between right and wrong is easy. We may not have the courage and confidence to *do* what is right, but that is a different matter. Yet if we can see what is right and wrong, then it is up to us to try our best to do the right thing and so help in the battle against evil.

You Can Make a Difference

We would like to imagine that our own lives aren't really part of the great battle. We wish to be left on our own. We want to mind our own business. We don't think our own little lives are particularly selfish and we don't see why our personal choices should make much difference.

When faced with this complacency in my own life I try to turn around and ask myself why I should be exempt from the battle. Can I really stand by and do nothing? If there is a great struggle between good and evil can I just hope for a quiet life and hope to avoid the conflict? What sort of a life is that? If I do not join in the battle, then I have wasted my life in easy comfort.

Instead of doing nothing, I should be using the life that has been given to me to make the world a better place. Each one of us wants life to have a purpose and meaning. The greatest purpose is the fight against evil. Do we want to change the world? We must begin by changing ourselves. Do we think we are too small to make a difference? The world has always been changed by individuals, not by committees. There is a great and eternal destiny for each one of us if we will only join the battle.

You Do Not Fight Alone

The encouraging thing in this battle is that we do not fight alone. Every other human being is also engaged in the fight. In the midst of our ordinary, mundane lives we may not see the reality of this, but it is true: every person you meet is fighting the shadows or giving in to the shadows a little bit more every day.

Terrible situations in war and extreme social conditions show that the vast majority of human beings want to fight on the right side. No matter what their religion or belief system, most people understand the simple decent thing to do. Most people want to stand up for the right when they have the chance.

As a result, when you decide to enter the battle actively you will find that you are fighting alongside a whole host of other people. Human beings from every nation, and from every religion and from every class of life will be there on your side fighting for honesty, justice, peace, prosperity, and goodness.

They do not only fight in the realm of ideas and great projects. The real battle goes on in the nitty-gritty of everyday life. Those who are engaged in the battle know that the front line is in the home, the workplace, the schools, and the community where they live. The war is huge, but every soldier contributes in his own humble way.

Christians believe that joining in this fight against evil is at the very heart of their own religious commitment. When people are baptized, they not only affirm their belief that Jesus Christ is the Son of God, and that he died for them; they also promise to fight against sin, the world and the devil. The Christian commitment is a commitment to stand up and fight..

Christians commit themselves to the battle for life. As they do, they join an army of others within their own community, around the world and down the ages who have also seen where the battle lines are and joined in to fight the good fight.

Chapter Two
The Armies of Darkness and Light

Two Levels of Battle

Every day when we watch the news or open a paper we are confronted with the reality of the fight between good and evil. The fight is there in almost every report if you have eyes to see it. This is the physical, historical dimension to the battle between good and evil: war, crime, conflict, injustice.

The battle is going on at a deeper level at the same time. At this level the struggle is spiritual and moral— not just physical and historical.

Because we human beings are both physical and spiritual it is possible for us to join in the battle in two different ways. We can fight on the side of goodness and light through our physical actions by doing good in the world, but we can also join in the spiritual battle against the forces of evil.

Christianity is a practical religion. It works. It helps us fight the battle against evil on both levels at the same time. An active Christian does not simply pray about the troubles in the world and then do nothing. Neither does he simply work hard to make the world a better place. Instead the active Christian prays hard and works hard. He uses both physical weapons and spiritual weapons in the battle against evil.

The Enemy is Real

God and the devil. Good and evil. Darkness and light. This is not just fantasy language or a symbolic way of looking at the world. The battle is real. Evil is real. Furthermore, that evil is planned and accomplished by real personalities. This is true on both the physical and spiritual levels.

When we consider the crimes committed by Hitler, Stalin, or Osama bin Laden; when we consider the crimes of a serial rapist or a sadistic child killer we know that there are some people who have given themselves to evil. These human beings are the physical perpetrators of evil.

There are spiritual agents of evil as well. Down through ages, in every society there is evidence of malignant forces—spiritual beings who are totally twisted by evil. Christians believe there are creatures who exist in a purely spiritual dimension. The good ones are called angels and the ones who have fallen into evil are called demons.

These evil spirits infest the world. They tempt people to commit crimes. If invited in, they can take over people's personalities and commit terrible atrocities through them. There is plenty of evidence from all over the world to show that these evil spirits do exist and can really influence individual lives and world events.

As a result, when we enter the battle against evil we will be opposed by evil human beings, but we will also be opposed by evil spiritual forces. We fight against the two different forces with different weapons. We use physical means to fight the physical battle, but we must use spiritual means to combat spiritual enemies.

Secret Allies

Sometimes it might look like the forces of evil are winning, but those who fight within the Christian Church are fighting on the side that has already won. When Jesus Christ rose from the dead, death and evil were defeated. The war has not yet been completed, but the seed of evil's defeat has been planted.

When Jesus Christ founded the Church he said "the gates of hell will never be able to prevail against it." In other words, those who follow Christ may lose some battles, but they cannot lose the war. As a result, when we become Christians and join the Church we join a company of triumphant warriors.

In this battle the Christian has three types of secret allies that the forces of darkness have not reckoned with. First of all, when a person becomes a Christian he immediately joins a whole range of fellow fighters across the world. All those who also follow Christ become his brothers and sisters. They also become his fellow foot soldiers. Like him, they are committed to the battle and fight by his side.

A Christian is also joined by the vast multitude of Christians who have left this physical life, but still live in the spiritual realm. All those who have died in the faith of Christ still live in his victory. They are still interested and involved in the battles going on here on earth. When Christians love and pray to those people, called the saints, they are enlisting their help for the ongoing battle.

Those who fight for the right also have the help of the spiritual powers who are on the side of goodness and light. Angels are God's messengers. They are also our helpers. In the spiritual battle they are committed to strengthening, guiding, and protecting us in the battle.

We do not fight alone. The angels and our fellow Christians—both alive and dead in Christ—fight by our side.

Physical Weapons, Spiritual Battlegrounds

Our bodies are our physical weapons in the battle. The New Testament says our bodies "are the temple of the Holy Spirit." In other words, our bodies are the special dwelling place of the Holy Spirit, and it is through our bodies that the Holy Spirit of Christ can conduct his battles against evil.

Our hands therefore can become the hands of Christ in the world. Our lips can speak his words and our feet can run to do his will. With our bodies we live and move in the physical realm and with our bodies we fight in the spiritual battle. When we help the sick, feed the hungry, or visit the prisoner, we are using our bodies to fight evil. Our bodies are not simply shells for our souls. Our soul does not inhabit a body as a person sits inside a car. Instead our bodies and souls are united in a single being. Our souls reside in our bodies more as water in a sponge than water in a cup. Because of this, our spiritual health and our physical health are interlinked.

What we do with our bodies, therefore, can affect the state of our souls; and likewise, what we do with our souls can affect the state of our bodies. It will be difficult to pray and worship, for instance, if our bodies are addicted to the poison of bad food, bad drugs, alcohol, or tobacco smoke. It will also be impossible to pray and worship if our minds are full of hatred and vengeful thoughts, envy, pornographic images, greedy ambitions, fear, and pride.

Likewise, what we do with our souls has an impact on our bodies and minds. If we pray, if we submit to God's way, if we ask for the Holy Spirit to fill our lives and guide us, then we will benefit physically and mentally. Many studies have shown that religious people live longer, and are generally happier. People who pray and meditate enjoy better health, have better marriages, heal faster, and are more optimistic about the future.

Spiritual Weapons

It is easy to forget that there is also a spiritual dimension to the battle against evil. It is easy to imagine that we can do nothing worthwhile in the spiritual realm. This is not so. We can have great spiritual power, and use that power for good.

The way to develop that spiritual power is to ask to be filled with the Holy Spirit. The Holy Spirit enables us to understand the rules of battle. The Spirit helps us discern the best way to fight, and where to focus our energy. The Holy Spirit also gives us the spiritual energy to take up the fight.

We stay tuned in to the Holy Spirit through prayer, meditation, contemplation and worship. Prayer is focused spiritual energy. Prayer is a way to align our will with God's will in order to accomplish great things in the spiritual realm. I will say more about prayer later, but it is enough at this point to say that there are many different forms of prayer, and each person needs to find what works best.

Chapter Three
The Most Powerful Weapons

The Physical/Spiritual Weapons

Because we are both spiritual and physical creatures
we fight the battle against evil in both spiritual and
physical ways. Physical actions against evil are the
good deeds that we do. Spiritual actions are prayer,
meditation, and worship.

But it is artificial to separate the spiritual from
the physical. Within us the spiritual and physical
dimensions are totally one. Our physical actions have
spiritual meaning and our prayers, involve our bodies.
One of the results of God taking human form in Jesus
Christ is that the barrier between the spiritual and
physical realms was broken forever.

In Jesus the spiritual and the physical are perfectly
united. If we are to become more like Jesus, then we
should be moving closer to that same unity between
the physical and spiritual realms. This is part of the

battle against evil. Those who are given to evil are deeply divided within, and their spiritual and physical natures are at war. Those who are moving towards goodness are also moving towards wholeness and inner unity. When we pursue the good we are also working to unify our spiritual and physical dimensions.

To bring us into this unity Christians have been given special weapons for the battle that combine the spiritual and the physical in one action. These weapons are called *sacraments*. The word "sacrament" is related to the word "covenant." A covenant is a solemn promise between two parties that is sealed by a physical action. So, for example, a marriage covenant is sealed with rings, or a peace treaty might be sealed with a ceremony in which swords are exchanged then solemnly broken.

In a sacrament we participate in a solemn ceremony which is physical and spiritual at the same time. The physical aspect of the sacrament makes real what it symbolizes spiritually. For example, when two people physically make love, that physical action seals their marriage and a physical/spiritual bond is established between them.

The same is true of all the sacraments. They are formal, solemn ceremonies in which a physical action effects and transforms our spiritual condition. As a result, sacraments are extremely powerful weapons in the ongoing battle against evil.

There are many physical actions and objects that can carry spiritual meaning and affect our spiritual condition. Candles and icons, holy buildings and sacred

sites, beautiful music, architecture, and paintings can
all have a wonderful spiritual effect. The beauties of
nature, the love of our families, and the simple physical joys of life can all help us and strengthen us in
the battle. But there are seven particular things that
Christians recognize as having a formal sacramental
effect in our life.

Joining and Belonging

On the Day of Pentecost, Jesus' followers received the
gift of the Holy Spirit. Peter was their appointed leader,
and when he stood up to speak he explained to the
crowd that to follow Christ they need to turn away from
their selfish ways, believe in Christ and be baptized.

Cleansed and Reborn

Baptism is the first sacrament of the Christian life.
When a person is baptized there is a spiritual dimension: faith, and a physical dimension: being put into
water. Being plunged into water symbolizes cleansing, but it also symbolizes re-birth. In addition, it
represents the fact that by believing in Christ we are
plunged into his death and resurrection.

If we are baptized as an adult then we make our
own declaration of belief in Christ. This is called a
"profession of faith." When a baby is baptized the profession of faith is made on his behalf by his parents
and sponsors (godparents).

As the person is plunged into the water or has water poured over him, the person performing the baptism proclaims that this solemn action is done in the name of the Father, the Son, and the Holy Spirit. This is to show that through baptism we enter into the very life of God himself, and God's life enters into us.

The sacrament of Baptism cleanses us from that inborn tendency to do wrong called original sin. It also gives us the power to live God's way and decide to follow his will in our lives. At that point the Holy Spirit begins to work in our lives to enable us to take part in the great battle against evil, sin, and death.

Sealed in Faith

The sacrament of *Confirmation* is when a baptized person is formally received into the Church. After a suitable time of instruction the baptized person decides that he wants to be a full member of the Church. At that point the Church leader (usually the bishop) lays his hands on the person's head and anoints him with blessed oil. This formal blessing symbolizes the father's blessing of his child, and through this physical/spiritual action a person is made a full member of the Church family.

What was begun at Baptism is completed at Confirmation. At that point the person makes sure or "confirms" his earlier decision, or the decision that was made for him by his parents if he was baptized as an infant.

Forgiven and Freed

At Baptism God cleanses us from original sin and gives us the power to fight the good fight of faith. But in that war we often lose some battles. It is not easy to follow Christ, and we fight against powerful enemies. The spiritual forces of darkness will do their best to make us fall into selfishness and sin.

We also have to fight against our own fallen nature. Baptism gives us the power to fight, but it doesn't mean we are made perfect overnight. Our own effort, co-operating with the power of the Holy Spirit, is required if we are to win the battle.

When we fail, members of our team pick us up and help us keep going. Remember, we are fighting as part of a great army, and it is part of an army's duty to set up ambulances, rescue teams, and field hospitals to help those who have fallen in battle. When we fall back into the darkness of selfishness, lust, anger, and violence, we have a way back into a good relationship with God. *Forgiveness* is God's way of putting us back into the same clean and whole condition we first received at our Baptism.

We receive God's forgiveness through the sacrament of *Reconciliation* or *Confession*. Confession is a powerful weapon in the battle against evil. At that point we speak to a priest. We simply tell him what we have done wrong and ask him to pray with us for God's forgiveness.

Jesus gave his disciples the power to forgive sins on earth just as he had done, and that power continues to be present and available to us through the ministry of the priest in the sacrament of Reconciliation. After we confess our sins to God the priest, by the power Christ gave the Church, solemnly pronounces God's forgiveness. This pronouncement is called "absolution." Through that gift we get a fresh start, the power to change and continue our fight against evil.

Healing, Inside and Out

When Jesus was on earth his power to forgive was always linked with his power to heal. Since the Church is the body of Christ on earth, the Church still has the power to do what Christ did. The Church is our army in the battle. She is there not only to equip us for battle, but to heal us when we're wounded.

In a general way we can be healed through medical technology and the work of professional physicians, but along with this obvious form of healing are some wonderful aspects of healing within the ministry of the Church. Some people in the Church have a counseling ministry. These people help us to find inner healing. Others have the ministry of spiritual direction. They help us to find spiritual healing and strength. Still others have the gift of physical healing.

There is also a formal sacrament of healing: the *Anointing of the Sick*. In this sacrament the physical element is blessed oil. The spiritual element is turning from our own way and having faith in Christ's healing power. The formal sacrament of healing is usually reserved for cases of extreme illness, and many priests and people report that real, physical healing often takes place when the sacrament is administered.

In other cases people are healed in an inner way. They may find new relief from pain, greater peace of mind, and a new strength to cope with their illness. Often the family members of the one who is anointed also find new strength and spiritual help in their time of need.

When a person is anointed at the very end of his life it is sometimes called *"Extreme Unction"* or *"The Last Rites."* Sometimes the sacrament helps bring the person back from death's door for a longer period of life. More often the last rites prepare the person for a peaceful death and assure him that his sins are forgiven, that all shall be well, and that he can depart in peace.

Forming a New Squadron

In every army there are subgroups—small, united, well-bonded fighting units. This is not a bad way to think of a Christian family. God loves to work through the power of human love and family ties. When a man, a woman, and children are bound together in the deep and abiding love of *marriage* they make up a powerful fighting force.

The powers of evil hate pure, solid, and sensible family love. That is why they tempt us with sexual sin —because they do not want us to be part of a happy marriage. They do not want children born into the world if they are going to be born into a solid, faithful Christian family.

Christians have always been devoted to building up the family. The sexual instincts are a powerful force. Through them love is expressed and comes to abundance in the lives of new children. Within a Christian marriage and family life there is great fruitfulness, great power for good, and therefore a great potential for victory over evil. Forming a Christian marriage is therefore one of the best ways anyone can fight against the powers of evil in the world.

That is why the Church has said that Marriage is a sacrament. In marriage the physical and the spiritual are joined in a marvelous and miraculous way. When a husband and wife make love they are sealing with a physical action a union that is spiritual and eternal. When they conceive, bear, and raise up children they are fostering new human beings with immortal souls, made in God's image.

Taking Orders

In the Christian battle there are some people who are professional soldiers. These are the ones who are uniquely dedicated to the battle. They have no other claims on their time. They are the specialists and the experts. They are available to go anywhere and serve God totally in the battle against evil.

When a man is ordained as a priest, or when a man or woman becomes a monk or a nun, they are specially dedicated to serve God only. This is why in most cases they also take a vow of celibacy. The vow of celibacy doesn't mean they think sex is wrong. They believe sex is wonderful, but that it belongs to marriage and family life. Because they have decided to serve God alone, they have given up family life and therefore have given up sexual relationships.

The formal sacrament of ordination, or *Holy Orders*, is reserved for men who are called by God and his church to be priests. The priesthood is reserved to men not because women are inferior, but because different roles are appropriate for men and women. In fact, all of us have different roles to play within the army of the church. In a sense all Christians are called to be "priests" because all of us are called to fight the good fight of faith and minister God's love to the world. However, while we all have a priestly type of ministry, we are not all *ordained* as priests because within the battle we exercise our priesthood in a multitude of different ways.

When a priest is ordained, the bishop and other priests lay hands on his head and he is anointed with oil for his new role in life. This is the physical aspect of the sacrament. The spiritual element is the man's calling, dedication to service, and faithful vow to serve Christ.

In each of these sacraments we are given a physical/spiritual weapon to help us in our physical/spiritual lives. The seven sacraments are God's way of helping us through every stage and decision point in our lives. From Baptism as an infant through Confirmation, Marriage, Reconciliation, and final Last Rites the Church, like an army or like a faithful family, is there to help us in the journey and equip us for the battle at hand.

But you may have noticed that I spoke of seven sacraments and only discussed six. The seventh is the greatest and needs a separate section of its own.

Chapter Four

The Ultimate Weapon

The Last Supper

There is one physical/spiritual weapon that is the greatest of all. In the last week of his life, Jesus gathered his apostles together and celebrated a special ceremonial meal with them.

As we discussed earlier, when the Jewish people were enslaved in Egypt God told them to sacrifice a young lamb and put the blood on the doorposts and lintels of their houses. When the angel of death saw the blood he would pass over their homes and spare them. Forever after that the Jewish people celebrated the same "Passover" meal every year. The killed a lamb, which they called "the Lamb of God, and as they ate the ceremonial meal, they re-lived their salvation from death and their delivery from slavery.

Jesus' last meal with his apostles was at the same time as this Passover meal. At the meal they read the

Old Testament story of the Passover, then celebrated the meal once again. At the meal they not only ate the lamb that had been sacrificed, they also ate bread and drank wine. As they shared this ancient ceremonial meal Jesus added a new dimension to it.

Jesus took the bread, blessed it, and broke it. He then said, "This is my body which is given up for you. Do this in remembrance of me." Then he took the chalice, blessed the wine and said, "This is my blood of the new covenant. Drink this in remembrance of me."

Remember the word "covenant" means sacred promise or a solemn agreement between two parties. John the Baptist had called Jesus the Lamb of God, and there at the Passover supper Jesus said he was going to die for his friends. *He* was therefore the Lamb of God who would be killed to deliver them from death and slavery. The old covenant was centered around the ritual sacrifice of animals in the Temple. Jesus inaugurated the New Covenant by sacrificing himself—one time for all humanity—on the Cross.

Jesus transformed the Jewish ceremonial meal into a new kind of meal. The new ritual would be not to commemorate the ancient delivery from slavery and death, but the delivery from slavery and death that he was to accomplish. Likewise he transformed the Temple sacrifice into a new kind of sacrifice, carried out on the altar at Mass and in the temple of our bodies. Jesus told his apostles to celebrate this physical/spiritual covenant, or sacrament, until the end of time.

I Am With You

Jesus also promised his apostles that he would be with them until the end of time. After he rose from the dead his apostles realized that he was with them in a powerful, new way through the ceremonial meal that he had commanded them to continue.

In a disturbing lesson, Jesus had told his followers that they could not have life within them unless they ate his flesh and drank his blood. Obviously he was not telling them to be cannibals, so what could he possibly have meant? It all came clear when he celebrated the Passover meal with them. When he said the bread was his flesh and the wine was his blood they remembered that he had said they couldn't have spiritual life within them unless they ate his flesh and drank his blood.

This same ceremonial meal-sacrifice has been continued for the last 2,000 years. In a multitude of ways all over the earth every day this sacred meal is celebrated with reverence, devotion, and care. Why do Catholics take such care and spend so much time on this ancient ceremony involving bread and wine?

It is because we really believe that Jesus Christ who lived and died and rose again is with us through the bread and wine. In fact, we believe that the bread and wine have been transformed into his body and blood. We do not believe that if you took the bread and wine into a laboratory it would turn out to be human flesh and blood. Instead, we believe that its inner reality

187

is transformed by God's power into Jesus' flesh and blood, his soul and divinity. One way to explain what we believe happens is to say that the bread's "bread-ness" and the wine's "wine-ness" has become the flesh and blood of Jesus Christ.

The sacraments are physical/spiritual realities. They are not just symbols. They are not just good ideas. We have bodies and souls blended together. Both are real. Therefore, God chooses to work in us through real bread and real wine that have been transformed by Christ's action into his own body and blood.

Battle Rations

Every army needs battle rations. Every pilgrim needs food for the journey. In *The Lord of the Rings* the travelers are given a special bread called *lembas* that never gets stale and gives them supernatural endurance. In the Old Testament exodus story the Jewish people were given *manna*—a special bread from heaven for their journey through the wilderness. When he was on earth Jesus fed a crowd by miraculously multiplying bread and fish.

When Jesus told his apostles to celebrate the memorial meal, the sacrificial ritual, until the end of time, he was commanding them to provide supernatural food for the troops. The successors of the apostles are the bishops and priests of the Church. By a direct historical line every Catholic priest can trace the fact that through his ordination he is descended from the

apostles. Because of this, he is the one who is autho-
rized to preside at the celebration of this ceremonial
meal which is called the Eucharist or the Mass.

The bread and wine do not become Christ's body
and blood by the priest alone. Instead the risen
and present Lord Jesus Christ performs the miracle
through the priest. When he does so we receive our
physical/spiritual food for the journey. When we eat
the bread and wine that have been transformed into
Christ's body and blood we receive Christ in a unique
and powerful way. The elements enter our body and
our bloodstream and we receive physical/spiritual
strength from them.

Christ is with us in this way more powerfully and
wonderfully than we ever could have imagined. This is
not simply a religious symbol or a spiritual idea. It is
a *reality*. Many Christians will relate how the spiritual
strength conferred by the Eucharist has helped them
make their way through life.

The Power to Change

It has been said, "you will become like the thing
you worship." This assumes that all of us worship
something; but often we are not aware of what we
worship. The way to figure out what we worship is to
ask ourselves what it is that we live for and what it is
that we would be willing to die for. That is the thing
we worship.

Do we worship our job? We might think that we are not willing to die for our boss, but if we devote the sort of lifestyle to our job that is slowly killing us, then maybe we are willing to die for our job. Do we worship the money that our job brings? Do we worship pleasure? If we are willing to risk our lives for that pleasure, (through smoking, overindulgence, promiscuous sex, or drugs) then we are willing to die for that thing.

Jesus Christ simply asks us to get our priorities right and to worship the only One who is worthy of our worship—and that is God. The word "Eucharist" means "thanksgiving," and when we go to the Eucharist we are worshipping God and giving thanks for all that he had done in our lives.

We do this by worshipping Jesus Christ who is God in human form. If you become like the thing you worship, then we choose to worship Jesus Christ because, as the God-Man, he is the one we want to be like. As we receive him into our lives by eating his body and drinking his blood at the Eucharist we really do receive the power to become like him.

This is what worship is all about, and by focusing on Christ at the Eucharist we immediately put all other false objects of worship into their rightful place. That's why we are expected to go to Mass every week— because we need a constant correction of our priorities. To fight well, we need to get focused and get our bearings time and time again.

Getting Focused

When we attend Mass every week we focus on the reason we're on this earth. We don't go for sensual pleasure. We don't go for financial profit. We don't go to fulfill some arbitrary religious requirement, and try not to be bored. We go for a purpose. We go to join in the fight against the powers of darkness and evil.

We cannot do this unless we bind ourselves to Christ, who already won the victory against evil. We do this first in Baptism and Confirmation, but we also renew our covenant with Christ through the sacrament of Reconciliation, and by receiving Communion regularly.

At Mass several passages from the Bible are read. The priest speaks for a short time to give us advice in the physical/spiritual battle we are a part of. The Bible is God's word to us. When we hear the Bible at Mass we are receiving spiritual food for our mind and soul.

After that, the priest performs a ritual recalling the Last Supper and Christ's sacrifice on the cross, and then we all celebrate the holy meal together. Just as Christ did, the priest takes the bread, breaks it, and blesses it. He then gives it to us as food for the journey, and as the living presence of Christ in our lives.

This sacrament is central to the lives of all Catholics since our faith is first and foremost about staying in touch with Christ, and keeping his Spirit alive inside us. Receiving him in this physical/spiritual way at Mass is the most vibrant, real and powerful way to stay in touch with him.

Taking Action

The sacraments are our weapons in the battle. They equip and strengthen us for the battle, but the battle is fought in our ordinary lives. Within our daily lives there are many ways to fight the battle, and I would now like to turn from the weapons to the battle itself.

Chapter Five

Changing Yourself

Good In Means Good Out

Your spiritual life is like a mill. You put grain in and you get flour out. If you don't put something good in, then you can't get something good out. It's as simple as that. Our minds need to be filled with good things if our lives are going to produce a good product.

In our media-saturated world it is difficult not to have our minds filled with lots of images and sounds. Of course, much of the content of popular music, television, films, and magazines is simply harmless fun. It entertains and amuses us, and that's good. But some of it is garbage: worthless trivia that occupies space on our mind's hard drive that should be used for something better; or worse, genuine trash that poisons our imagination and pollutes our minds with violent, pornographic, or materialistic images and desires.

If we are fighting a spiritual battle, then we will make sure that we fill our minds instead with things that are good, true, and beautiful. We should take time for the natural goodness of the world around us. We should open our minds to the best music, literature, and art. We should learn to enjoy all that builds us up and opens our minds to the best in other cultures. One of the best ways to win this aspect of the battle is to take time to read good books that engage the mind with ideas in a fresh way.

For a Christian, one of the key sources of learning and enlightenment is the documents of the faith. The writings of the saints, the words of worship, and the Bible all contribute to building up the mind and putting in goodness so goodness can come out.

The Good Book

The Bible is made up of two main sections: the Old Testament and the New Testament. The Old Testament records the religious history of the Jewish people as well as their religious poetry, sayings, sermons, and hymns. The New Testament begins with four versions of the story of Jesus Christ, called the gospels. The rest of the New Testament is the story of the foundation of the Christian Church and letters of instruction that the apostles wrote to the first Christians.

Christians believe that the Bible is *inspired* by God. This doesn't mean we believe it dropped out of heaven. Nor was it dictated to the human writers by an angel or the Holy Spirit. Instead, the Holy Spirit inspired or "breathed into" the writers in a more subtle way. The Holy Spirit infused the Biblical authors with the insights and ideas he wanted to communicate, and the power to express them properly. We also believe that the same Holy Spirit uses the Bible today to inspire and enlighten us as we read it.

Pick Up and Read

Therefore every Catholic should have a Bible and read it. It is difficult, however, to decide how and when to read the Bible. Some people simply start at the beginning and read a chapter a day. But the most difficult parts of the Bible are at the beginning, and many people get bogged down after only a week or two.

The best way of reading the Bible is to read it with the whole Church, day by day and week by week. When we go to Mass, a section of the Old Testament, an ancient Jewish hymn called "a psalm," and a section of the New Testament is read. Then a portion from one of the gospels is read. All these weekly portions are collected in a book called a missal. If you have a missal you will have handy and accessible portions of the Bible to read day by day and week by week.

Other people use Bible reading guides, often published in little magazines that you can buy in Christian bookstores or order by mail. These give you a portion of the Bible to read every day and provide a few paragraphs to explain the Bible passage and apply it to your life.

It is possible to study the Bible in great depth, or simply to read it to learn more about your faith. But either way the Bible is best read in an atmosphere of prayer. You should ask the Holy Spirit to open your eyes to the truths in the Bible and to help you understand what you read and apply it in your life. The wisdom and the words of the Bible do have a power to transform lives, and if you want to get energy and light for the battle against the darkness, then read the Bible and learn how to pray.

Keeping in Touch

Prayer is absolutely vital not just when reading the Bible, but for the whole spiritual life. No one can grow as a a follower of Christ without learning how to pray, and we learn how to pray as we learn how to swim or ride a bike—by regular practice.

Many people's ideas of prayer are linked with a childhood understanding of prayer. They imagine that prayer consists of asking God for things they want. Certainly there is one dimension of prayer that consists of asking God for what we want, but prayer is much greater than that. Someone has well said, "prayer doesn't change God, it changes me."

In other words, we pray first and foremost to align ourselves with God's will. When Jesus taught his disciples to pray he instructed them to say to God, "May your will be done on earth as it is in heaven." In other words, they were subjecting their own will to God's will. Through prayer they were trying to find out what God wanted—not tell him what *they* wanted. That's why, when a Christian asks God for anything he ends the request by saying, "If it is your will."

So real prayer is asking God for the things that are his will. You might then ask, what is the point? If it is his will won't it happen anyway?

When we pray we align our will with God's. We submit our understanding and our wishes to his. His will in the world is constant, huge and active. It involves all things and knows all things. When we say, "Thy will be done" it is as if we are fitting ourselves into that greater action of God. We are "going with God" not doing it all ourselves. If you look at it this way, prayer is like surfing. God's will is the big wave coming in. I am trying to find out where it's going, then to go with it and ride the wave. When I align my life and my will with what God is doing all things become possible.

Purifying the Mind

Many religions teach their followers to meditate. Meditation is known to have many practical beneficial effects. People who meditate regularly have less stress. They live longer. They are happier and they deal with problems in a more confident way. People who meditate enjoy better health, better relationships and a better quality of life.

In the Eastern religions the meditation technique is to empty the mind and simply dwell in the eternal silence. This activity slows down the mind waves and allows the person who is meditating to enter into a calmer, more peaceful state of being.

For Catholics, meditation is different. Catholics use the word "meditation" for another kind of mental activity. When Catholics meditate they take a story from the gospels or a word or phrase from the Bible and they "bathe themselves" in that idea, phrase, or mental image. They relax into the particular phrase or idea or image until it goes deep into them and they become part of it.

Many Catholics use the rosary as a way of doing this. The rosary is a pattern of repetitious prayers, kept track of by holding a string of beads in the fingers. These prayers help to calm the mind and take the person to a deeper state of consciousness. At the same time, a person is expected to focus on a particular event in the life of Jesus. As we say the prayers and enter into this deeper state we also enter more deeply into the life, ministry, death, and resurrection of Jesus. In this way our life is merged with his life and we become more like him.

This is a more positive and objective form of meditation than the Eastern religions practice. It doesn't call for an empty mind and a focus on nothingness, but for a mind full and focused on real and powerful content. Christian meditation is just as calming and peaceful as Eastern meditation, but it is also meaningful, and as such it is a simple and effective way to get closer to Christ and engage in the spiritual battle against evil.

The Still Point of the Turning World

Contemplation is the form of prayer for Catholics that is most like meditation in the Eastern religions. In contemplative prayer a person is taken beyond meditation on a particular image, phrase, or story. When a person enters into contemplation he simply dwells in the presence of Christ. This sounds rather strange. It isn't. Have you ever spent an evening with someone you love and realize that you don't have to talk or play a game or go out somewhere? It is fine to simply be together. Maybe you are reading together or doing a puzzle or knitting. You don't need to talk to one another. You can simply "be" together.

Contemplation is like that, except that the other person we are with is Jesus Christ. In the forms of meditation taught by the Eastern religions the person meditating is supposed to empty his mind, but in Christian contemplation we fill our mind with the presence of Christ.

An old peasant woman was asked how she prays. She said, "I just sit and look at Him and he sits and looks at me." That simple peasant was a real contemplative, and her words fit in with the experience of millions of Christians. The greatest saint of modern times, a young French woman named Thérèse Martin said that contemplation was to "gaze on the face of Christ."

Another way to "gaze on the face of Christ" is in the traditional time of prayer called "adoration of the

Blessed Sacrament." In this simple act of worship the consecrated bread from the Eucharist is displayed on the altar in a large receptacle called a monstrance. The simple white disc which is truly the body of Christ becomes the focus point for our contemplation, and through this action we enter into his presence in a way far beyond all words and description.

Communities of Prayer

Prayer is so important to the spiritual struggle that there are communities of people who live together to devote their lives entirely to prayer. Monks and nuns give up all other ambitions to spend their whole lives in prayer.

This doesn't mean they spend every moment of every day on their knees in church. Instead they try to live a life in which prayer is the heartbeat of every moment. Monks and nuns *do* spend much time in actual prayer, but they are also trying to bring prayer into every moment of life so that every action and thought also becomes totally given to God, and so becomes a kind of prayer.

There are a large number of different communities of prayer all over the world. Some are for men only, some for women only. Some have married couples and families living together with celibate people. Some are totally enclosed and traditional. In these communities the men and women rarely go out and pursue a totally inner life of study and prayer.

Other communities are more open and are engaged in activities to promote the Christian faith, work for justice and peace, and to help the disadvantaged, disabled, and poor. In these communities the devoted men and women combine prayer with action in a life of total dedication.

These special communities are part of the whole Church, but each local church or parish is also supposed to be a community of prayer. As we meet together with one another and in our own homes, we are constantly fighting the battle against evil by learning how to pray.

Getting Together

The local community gets together every week to do together what each Catholic should have been doing on his own throughout the week. At Mass we pray, read the Bible, focus on Christ, and re-commit ourselves to the battle we first signed up to in our baptism.

Catholic worship has a basic structure called the liturgy. This structure is provided by the Church, and it is the same basic structure that has been used for the last 2,000 years.

In this structure we do not use our own words to worship God, but the words that are shared by the whole of God's family. Using a set structure like this does two things. First it ensures that the words of worship are completely Catholic, and that they have not been infected with false ideas. Second, it binds us together with all other Catholics who have used, and are using, these same words.

While we use the same set structure, the actual worship may vary somewhat. The music and style of using these words can be very different depending on where you go. Therefore in one place the Mass may be a solemn High Mass with classical music and a fine choir. In another place the music will be provided by a group of local people playing instruments and singing simple hymns. If you go to Africa or South America the style will be very different still, but the basic structure and the content will be the same.

This unity in the midst of diversity is one of the great strengths of the Catholic Church. In it we can all worship the same Lord Jesus Christ. We can all commit to the same battle, and yet we can also be ourselves and worship God in a language and style that is right for us.

Chapter Six

Changing Your World

What's the Point?

Prayer, worship, and reading are not the end goal of
the practice of the Catholic faith. Like the sacraments
they are only the means to an end. We do these things
because they bring us into a closer relationship with
God, by whom our lives are transformed. By prayer,
worship, and the practice of religious sacraments God
works in our lives, and we gradually grow into the
people we were created to be.

Yet Christianity has never simply been about personal fulfillment or salvation. From the very beginning,
Christianity, like the Jewish faith from which it developed, has been a *communal* religion.

It is impossible to be a solitary Christian. To be
a Christian means we belong to the body of Christ
and that body is made up of all the other people in
the world and down the ages who have also followed

Christ. To be a Catholic means belonging to the Catholic Church: made up of all those alive in the world today and all those Catholics who have gone before us.

So, being a Catholic means we are involved with all other Catholics. But we are not only involved with other Catholics, we are also involved with all people. We are called to be concerned about their welfare and to do as much as we can to help them. We do not ask God to change us through prayer, worship, and personal renewal just for our own gratification. We ask him to change us so that we can also go on to change the world.

Missionaries of Charity

Mother Teresa of Calcutta was an excellent example of how prayer and action can go together. Mother Teresa was a nun. Her life was devoted to prayer, meditation, and contemplation. For many years she taught in a convent school for middle-class Indian girls. If Mother Teresa had only been interested in her own salvation she would not have had the eyes to see the suffering of others. But through her prayer she also became aware that she should be serving the poorest of the poor in the slums of Calcutta.

Eventually she founded a little community of women who were devoted both to prayer and to a ministry to the poorest of the poor. Mother Teresa and her nuns would start each day with an hour of meditation and then worship God at the Eucharist. Each working day was punctuated with times of prayer, reading, and contemplation.

In the middle of this life of prayer Mother Teresa
and her nuns were working. They were working tire-
lessly to comfort the poor and dying. Mother Teresa
said she *did* this because she saw the face of Christ in
every poor person. She could only recognize the face
of Christ in the poor because she had spent so long
gazing on the face of Christ in contemplation. Mother
Teresa and her nuns set an example for all Christians:
prayer is the engine for changing the world.

Haves and Have Nots

Mother Teresa's work is just one example of the
Catholic faith in action. There are thousands of examples of different ways that Catholics work out their own
salvation by ministering to others. Down through history more schools, hospitals, clinics, universities, and
food banks have been started and staffed by Catholics
than by all other groups put together. Driven by their
life of prayer, and motivated by the example of Jesus
Christ, Catholics have been at the forefront of the battle
against poverty, disease, and injustice in all its forms.

Those who work with the poor are the front-line soldiers. There are others who work from home adminis-
tering charities, educating the public about the needs of
the poor, and working hard not just to treat the symptoms, but to address the root problems of poverty.

This battle against poverty goes on in every country;
in the cities and in the countryside. It goes on where
famine and disaster strike and where ordinary conditions force people to live lives of misery and squalor.

If you want to change the world there are a multitude of ways for your Catholic faith to help you get involved and make a difference.

Peace and Justice

If Catholics are hard at work relieving poverty, they are also busy trying to establish peace and justice in the world, through social and political activism. This too, is the Catholic faith in action. Furthermore, the Catholic who prays and worships is committed to working for peace and justice *in his own life*. He should constantly ask himself if he is doing enough to live a simple life, to help the poor, and to exhibit love and kindness towards his family, friends, and neighbors.

Think what the world would be like if everyone were honest. Think what the world would be like if everyone did their best, never made a quarrel worse, and always sought for fairness and justice for all. What a wonderful world it could be!

We cannot make such a world overnight, but if every Catholic were to take their faith seriously and try even a little bit harder, then the world would be a better place for everyone.

Reconciliation and Forgiveness

I cannot change the world, but with God's help I can change myself. I cannot take away all the suffering and pain in the world, but I can start with the pain and suffering that I cause other people.

If a Catholic takes his faith seriously, then he must always be on the lookout for ways to make things better within his own life and within their own relationships. Our hearts are constantly tempted by jealousy, pride, envy, hatred, bitterness, and the desire for revenge. It is a Catholic's responsibility to address these problems in his own heart, in his own life, and in his own relationships.

If we were to allow the Holy Spirit to rule our lives and direct us, then we would have the courage to reach out to those who have offended us with forgiveness. We would have the courage to build new relationships of love and justice. We would have the insight to be happy with what we have rather than seeking for more, more, more.

The Catholic faith is practical. It works. All the religious activity is meant to get us to the point where Jesus Christ is so much a part of us that he works through us to bring about his will in the world. The battle against evil really can be won. Suffering really can be defeated. The world can be changed. And the change starts right where I am at this present moment in time.

Starting Where We Are

Mother Teresa started where *she* was. She was just another nun teaching in a school for girls. Once she got permission to start working among the poor she moved to a slum in Calcutta and did what she could do. She was a teacher. She started teaching the slum children. She didn't have any training as a nurse so she got some and started ministering to the health needs of the poor as well. Eventually some of her former students came to help her and the now famous-order of nuns came into being.

Each one of us can begin to change ourselves and to change the world, and we can start where we are. Every journey begins with the first step. It might seem that you are a nobody. Wonderful. It is always people who know they are nobody who change the world for the best. It might seem that you have no gifts. The best gifts are not wealth, education and brilliance, but a heart and mind totally transformed by the power of the Holy Spirit.

Right now, this very day you can decide to change yourself and follow Christ into the amazing future he has prepared for you. Right now, this very day you can decide to work with him to change the world as much as you can. Right where you are, you can decide to make the most of your gifts and the most of who you are and spend the rest of your life making the world a better place. Whoever you are, you can decide to fight the great fight against evil, or give in to that evil.

Climb Every Mountain

No one promises that the fight will be easy. Indeed, deciding to fight against evil and live for Christ is the most difficult thing you will ever decide to do. You will constantly stumble and fall in your effort to live a better life. You will be disappointed in yourself and disappointed with others.

If you decide to live the Christian life you will discover that the Church is full of hypocrites. Other

Christians will let you down. Some Church leaders will turn out to be sinners and shallow, self-centered frauds. Some of your friends will show themselves to be weak-willed, lazy, and unwilling to help in the battle. Then, if you have any insight, you will realize that they are all just like you.

Don't imagine that the Catholic life will be a nice, easy life full of wonderful spiritual experiences and "happy religious time." You will get discouraged. There will be dark times. Remember, you are engaged in a war. You may think at times that you will never win. You may despair as you lose battle after battle. You may be tempted to give up, and at the end you will be convinced that the darkness is greater than the light.

In fact, like climbing a mountain, the further you go on this journey, the harder it will become. But also like climbing a mountain, the further you go, the better the views get. The air is clearer, and you become stronger and more resolute.

Are you up to the challenge? As I've said, no one can do it alone. That is why we are accompanied and helped on the journey by all the others who have also decided to follow Christ. The final section of this book will help you explore the Church in more detail, and help you to understand more about the amazing army of God that becomes your new family.

SECTION FIVE

WELCOME HOME

Chapter One
The Family of God

The Homecoming

One of the most famous stories Jesus Christ told was about a runaway son. The boy went to his wealthy father and asked for his inheritance money early. The doting father gave him some cash and the boy ran off and wasted it on parties and pleasure.

When the money ran out the boy's friends ran out too. Hard times hit the city and soon the boy was stuck with no money, no friends, no qualifications and no future. He ended up taking a job as a pig farmer, and had to fight the pigs to get enough food to eat. Then he remembered his father.

At that point Jesus says the boy "came to himself." He saw himself and his circumstances as they really were. He realized how good he'd had it at home. Even his father's servants were better off than he was then. If he were to go home and volunteer to be a servant in his father's house perhaps he would at least have a decent meal every day.

The boy started on the long road home. As he approached he saw that his father was at the front gate waiting and watching for his return. The father rejoiced at his son's return, forgave him everything and welcomed him home with a great feast.

When a person decides to change his life and follow God's way instead of his own selfish way, it is just like the homecoming of that runaway son. Every time we take a step towards God and away from our own selfishness it is as if we have arrived home. Part of us is complete. A deep, dark corner of our lives is touched with light and we begin to glimpse the possibility of finding the peace we have always looked for.

Brothers and Sisters Abounding

The apostle Paul said that to come home like this was to become a member of the family of God. He recognized that all human beings are the fugitive sons and daughters of God, and that to be restored to the family we first have to turn towards home.

This is a *reality*, not just a theory or a nice way of talking about being religious. Once we turn from our way and accept Christ's way, once we believe that Jesus Christ died to give us new life, a real transformation takes place in our relationship with God. Like runaways we have come home, and the Father welcomes us with open arms. As the father did in the story, God then gives us a whole array of good gifts.

This new relationship with God means we also enter into a new relationship with every other person who has ever followed Jesus Christ down through the centuries. For 2,000 years people have taken the same decision. They have also heard God's call, and decided to leave everything and follow him. They too returned home and were welcomed into the family of God.

The Christians down through the ages are therefore our brothers and sisters. They are not alive on this earth, but they are alive on the other side, and they are interested in us and the rest of God's family. These people who have been totally transformed by Christ's loving power are the saints. In Christ they are our older brothers and sisters.

Making New Old Friends

The saints make up a vast and varied collection of people. There are saints from every walk of life, from every class, race, and nationality. Children, old people, soldiers, nuns, politicians, and priests have all become saints. Parents, husbands and wives, scholars and simpletons, princes and peasants have all become saints. The vast array of saints shows us that anyone who is willing can be totally transformed by Christ.

The Bible calls the saints a "great cloud of witnesses." The word used for "witness" is the same word for "martyr"; and in their own way all the saints have learned to give up their lives for Christ. Some of them literally gave up their lives at the hands of violent men. Others gave up their lives more quietly, in the service of others and in constant self-giving.

The saints still work with Christ for the redemption of the world even though they are in heaven, not on earth. As we fight the battle against evil we become aware that we do not fight alone. Our older brothers and sisters in the faith love us and fight with us in the great battle.

As we begin walking in the Christian life it will not be long before we learn more about certain saints. Their lives will appeal to us. We will want to learn more about how they followed Christ, and we will desire to follow their example. As we do, we will feel that the saints are with us as friends and fellow travelers in the journey.

Unity and Diversity

We can't see the saints, but we know they are with us because they are alive in God, and God is always with us. They are present during our prayers. They are present at the *Mass*, where we recognize their presence and pray with them. They are present with us as we contemplate their lives and deeds. We soon become aware that we do not worship alone, but we worship with a great cloud of witnesses surrounding us.

I mention the saints in heaven first because it is vital to remember that being a Christian joins us with a group of people who have been alive and active in the world for the last 2,000 years. What we do here and now is connected with what has gone before.

Once we are aware of our relationship with all the saints of the past we will better understand our relationship with all the other Christians in the present. When we become Catholic we do not simply join our local church. The Catholic Church is vast, and there is a huge variety of people and types of people within it all over the world. Just as there is a huge variety of saints, so there is a huge range of people who are Catholics in the world today.

Within the vast range of national groups, races, classes, and abilities there is yet a remarkable unity. Down through the ages, political rulers have tried to establish world wide power—an empire, political network or universal brotherhood that included all people. In the Catholic Church it already exists. Within the Church all people can exist together as brothers and sisters in Christ.

Groups and Sub-Groups

Because of the vast range of people in a local parish it's sometimes difficult to feel at home. A Catholic church sometimes feels more like a bus stop than a family gathering—a vast range of people gathered together for the same practical reason, who otherwise don't seem to belong together at all.

It is vital to take an active part in our local parish because that is where we learn to get along with other Catholics who may be very different from us. But it is also important to realize that within the Catholic

Church there are many smaller groups and sub-groups. If the Catholic Church is like a huge tree, then there are many different branches and twigs. Along with active parish involvement, many Catholics also find a group or sub-group within the Church where they find others with shared interests and outlooks.

There are groups for young people and groups for the elderly. Some nurture prayer, spirituality, Christian growth, and evangelization. Others focus on church worship and music. Some help build marriages and family life. Others are involved in education, health care, ecology, and concern for the poor. Still others look after children, foster adoption, and work to eliminate the crime of abortion. All these groups are Catholic. Some of them are well established. Others are exciting new movements in the Church. All of them focus on Jesus Christ in the Catholic Church, but they also have their own priorities, aims, and ways of working.

Parish life is where the ordinary day-to-day spiritual life takes place, and it mustn't be neglected, but seeking out one of the groups within the Catholic Church will help you feel at home. It will provide a way for your spiritual life will go forward by leaps and bounds. The others in that group will help you to feel part of the larger family, and as you get involved with them in the life of Christ you will realize that this kind of unity and commitment is what makes life worthwhile.

Fitting In, Not Sticking Out

It will not always be easy to stay with the Catholic Church. Sometimes other churches may seem more attractive and happier places to be. But joining the Catholic Church is a serious business. It is like marriage. You make the promises for better or for worse. It is not good flitting from one church to another any more than you should flit from one marriage to another.

Throughout one's relationship with the Church the difficulties are part of the larger test. This process helps us to grow spiritually. To be a Catholic means we accept that the Church is bigger, older, and wiser than we are. It means we don't set out to change the Church, but to allow the Church to change us. The Church was there before we were. We realize that the Church is the creation of Jesus and belongs to him.

A person does not join the Catholic Church because it is the church with the best music or the nicest people or the most interesting sermons. To tell you the truth, if you want nice music, go to a concert. If you want nice people, join the country club. If you want good speeches join a speaker's club. But if you want to belong to the fullest expression of the Body of Christ on earth, then become a Catholic.

Finding our place in the Church is a necessity because the whole point of the Christian life is to go with God. By fitting into our place in Church we put our own will to the side. We try to be humble and say, "Well, maybe I don't know best all the time. I'm going to try to learn

from the difficulty. I'm going to find God right here—
not somewhere else." At that point we start to learn that
God is best discovered by finding our rightful place
within the vast and beautiful unity that is the One, Holy,
Catholic, and Apostolic Church.

Chapter Two
One Church

Longing for Unity

When we perceive chaos and disorder in the world, it makes us frustrated and angry. It is part of human nature to want things to fit together. We want to find meaning in the universe. We want all that is broken to be mended, all that is wounded to be healed and all that is divided to be reconciled. In other words, we want *unity*.

Even within ourselves we long for unity. Our selfish ambitions clash with our spiritual goals. The desires of our body war against the better ideals of our soul. Our mental ideas and viewpoint don't fit the reality of life.

We also long for unity in our relationships. We want our families and friends to live together in peace and harmony, not in anger and bitterness. We also long for unity in our communities, our nation and our world. We don't want to see the destruction and division caused by war, violence, hatred, and selfishness.

This longing for unity reaches to the whole world. We want a system of belief that reconciles not only us, our friends, and our relationships, but the whole world. When we say that we believe in "one Church" we profess our belief that the unity we long for exists in the Christian Church. That unity is not perfect yet, but in the Church we can get a glimpse of the unity that all human beings should share.

One Lord, One Faith, One Baptism,

In the New Testament the apostle Paul said, "There is one Body, one Spirit, one Lord, one faith, one baptism," When we are baptized we enter into that one Body. We trust that one faith, and join our divided selves with this greater unity that exists within God's will. Elsewhere Paul said the Church is the Body of Christ, and that each member is a part of that body. Jesus himself said there would be "one flock and one shepherd."

Jesus wanted there to be one Church on earth, to be a source of reconciliation, unity, and peace for the whole of humanity. As individuals came into unity with Christ they were also coming into unity with one another, and with God's plan for the whole world. This unity is a vital sign that Jesus" message is true. Jesus prayed that his followers would be one as he and the Father are one. This unity had to be *visible* unity, because Jesus said others would see that unity and believe in him.

The Church is not just a club of like-minded religious people. It is more like a living organism, with its own mind and spirit and soul. That organism is united in the one faith that was given to it by Jesus Christ. All members of the organism are united by the fact that they share that faith and have been baptized into the new life of Jesus Christ. Each member everywhere in the world, from every race, language, tribe, and tradition, is united by their shared allegiance to Jesus Christ as their Lord and God.

This unity is not just a pretty word picture. It means I'm not alone. I'm a part of every other Christian I meet. I am not an island. I am a living cell in the great, cosmic, body of Christ on earth.

The Church's First Division

All Christians are united by our shared faith in Jesus Christ, and our baptism into his death and resurrection. This is a real and permanent unity that can never be destroyed. However, if the Church is the body of Christ, that body is wounded by division and strife. Not only is the body wounded; it still bleeds.

During the first thousand years of Christianity the Church was united. There were some breakaway groups though the centuries; there were some little factions that disagreed and separated themselves from the mainstream, but for the most part the Christian Church was united around a group of leaders with the Bishop of Rome, the Pope, as the recognized head.

The Church's life was closely bound up with the political life of the Roman Empire, and as the Roman

Empire crumbled and divided, the Christian Church also fell into opposing camps. Increasingly, the churches in the ancient Middle East and North Africa went their own way. Nevertheless, unity was retained under the leadership of the Bishop of Rome.

Then when the church was about one thousand years old, the conflict between the Eastern Churches in Greece, Turkey, the Middle East, and North Africa came to a head. They broke away from the ancient leadership of Rome. The Roman leaders and the Eastern Church leaders cut each other off and a major division in the Church took place. For complicated reasons the division still exists. Many Christians from the East—including Russia and parts of Eastern Europe—remain partially cut off from the rest of the Catholic Church.

We look to the Eastern Christians and admire them as our brothers and sisters in Christ. Like Catholics, they have retained the ancient faith that has been handed down to us from the first followers of Jesus called apostles. The Eastern churches have retained wonderful traditions and have endured terrible persecution. Catholics long for a reunion to take place so that the whole Church may once again breathe with two lungs of East and West.

The Reformation Divides Christians Further

Five hundred years after the Eastern and Western parts of the Church divided, another terrible separation took place. In the sixteenth century, Europe was going through a time of enormous social and technological upheaval. In some parts of the Catholic Church there was corruption, complacency, and confusion. In this midst of this confusion came new teachings that seemed to liberate individual Christians. Fiery preachers stirred the people up with a simplified gospel message that rejected what they considered false Church teachings (like belief in the Eucharist) and rituals they considered to be overly complicated and ornate.

At the same time new political forces were rising in Europe, that were at odds with the Church and jealous of her influence and wealth. The new religious thinkers joined forces with the new political leaders, and before long they had the power and support to start their own churches.

In Germany the Lutherans broke away from the ancient Church. In Switzerland the Calvinists (or Presbyterians) broke away. In England dissenting groups supported the king as he broke away to establish the Church of England. Later the Methodists broke away from the Church of England (Anglicans) The Baptists grew out of many other smaller and more extreme breakaway groups. Each religious teacher seemed to find something different in the Bible and ultimately they disagreed with one another and set out to start their own churches.

Now a directory of denominations in the USA lists over 20,000 different non-Catholic denominations. Surely this could not be what Christ intended when he founded one Church to reconcile all people and bring everyone into a new kind of unity for mankind!

A Wounded Church

It cannot be overestimated how much damage this division has caused the Church of Christ. The battle against evil is much more difficult if the soldiers of goodness are divided against themselves.

Catholics believe that all Christians who have faith in Christ and are baptized are in a real and substantial unity with them. However, they also recognize that the unity of Christ's Church is deeply wounded. Furthermore, the grievances of the past cannot be glossed over. We can't just pretend the problem doesn't exist.

When we honestly face the division in this way, we are not judging the goodness of other Christians. We are simply facing the reality that real divisions of belief and practice still exist among Christians, and problems don't go away by imagining that such differences aren't important. Instead Catholics are committed to work together with our separated brothers and sisters to solve the problems of a wounded Church through dialogue, forgiveness, and self-sacrifice.

Working Towards Unity

As Catholics it is important to work together with other Christians in the fight against evil. It is possible to work together with non-Catholic Christians in the areas

of spreading the faith, charity work, political involvement, social concerns, and regular prayer and worship.

On the formal level the Catholic Church is involved
in complicated discussions with a whole range of non-
Catholic Christians. Great progress is being made in
resolving differences, clearing up misunderstandings
and developing new trust and friendship.

The same is possible on the local and personal level.
In this age there is simply no room for Christians of
various traditions to be suspicious of one another.
Fighting amongst ourselves is a victory for the forces
of evil. All of us who follow Christ are called to unity
with him and unity with one another. The fact that this
unity has been broken only calls for us to work harder
to love and understand one another. Only in that way
can we all attain to the radiant goodness and the abundant life that Jesus Christ has to offer.

Chapter Three
Holy Church

Holiness and Wholeness

All of us are incomplete. There is so much we still have
to learn. There are huge gaps not only in our knowledge,
but also in our accomplishments. There is so much
we could do if we had the time, the self discipline and
the courage! Furthermore, there is a shadow side of us
which keeps us from fulfilling all that we could be.

A mature and whole person has realized that his
shadow side is a distorted part of his good side. Each
negative part of us is only the dark side of a genuine
strength. The mature person learns how to turn stub-
bornness into determination, lust into love, ambition
into positive power and greed into a desire for goodness.

This is what holiness is like. In fact the word "holiness" is linked to the word "wholeness." When a person is holy he is whole. He is complete, mature, fully
formed—all that he possibly could be. The warring

227

elements in his nature have been reconciled. Priorities have been established and he has learned to live at peace with himself, with God, and with others.

The Power of Perfection

We say the Church is "holy" not because everyone in it is perfectly saintly all the time. Anybody can see that isn't true. Instead we proclaim that the Church is holy because God's powerful grace is present in and through the Church at all times—because Jesus founded it and bound himself to it in love forever. This grace imbues the Church with a goodness and a power that is greater than the imperfections it is trying to overcome.

God's grace ministers to us through the Church as a mother helps, nurtures, and instructs her child. The child might be weak, but the mother's love is strong. We need that powerful force of goodness in our lives if we are to become like Christ. Without it we are simply trying hard to be nicer better people, and we won't really get that far. So as one wise writer observed, "It is impossible to have God as your Father if you do not have the Church as your mother."

Because the Church is like a mother to us we sometimes compare the Church to Jesus' mother Mary. Mary was a perfectly whole and complete person. She was holy in a natural, wise, and loving way. As she is the image of the perfectly loving and gentle mother, so she is also the image of the Church. As she nurtured Jesus, the Christian community becomes our teacher, our comforter, and our friend. As a mother the Church feeds us, supports us, and gives us a spiritual home.

As we receive God's grace within the Church we take great strides towards that wholeness that is called holiness. Those who are perfectly whole and complete in this way have great power. God radiates through their lives in an amazingly potent way. They can do great things. They can move mountains of resistance and difficulty. They can change the world. The Church is also "holy," then, because it empowers people like this.

The Problem of Imperfection

If you know anything about the Church you will protest, "Hold on a moment! The Christians I know aren't anything like that. They're a grumpy, narrow-minded group of people who are always fighting among themselves."

We should be willing to excuse the little imperfections of ordinary Christians. After all, nobody said we would be made perfect all at once. All of us are on a gradual learning curve. We're still taking the lessons and doing the practice. We might be on the right road, but we admit that we haven't arrived yet.

Of course, little imperfections are one thing, but what about the huge crimes committed by Christians —especially those committed by Christian leaders? What are we to think when we hear of sexually criminal priests, abusive nuns, and the corrupt, power-hungry popes from centuries ago? What can we say about the history of wars, imprisonment, torture, and executions conducted in the name of Christ?

There are two answers to the problem of imperfection amongst Christians. First, it is fair to remember that there is a war going on. There are forces that will do anything to destroy Christ and his Church. These powers will use the media to twist the truth and make problems seem worse than they are. To be fair we must read both sides of any story and really gather facts — not just propaganda. When we look at the facts fairly the wrongdoing is often not as bad as the propaganda would make out.

Nevertheless, there have been some monstrous crimes committed by Christians — including high-ranking Catholic leaders. It would be foolish to pretend otherwise. All we can say is that such crimes are not only terrible, but they are made worse because the person has professed to follow Jesus Christ. Nonetheless, it is possible to condemn the crimes of Christians but still admit the truth of their message. A murderer could preach a very convincing sermon against killing. When a person doesn't live up to the ideal it doesn't mean the ideal was wrong.

Don't Forget the War

Are you really surprised when good people do bad things? Good people are those who are most involved in the battle against evil, and in any war there will be some major casualties. Sometimes the enemy will win a battle (even though he will never win the war).

While God's grace is at work, human selfishness, greed, anger, and violence are also still at work. The war between good and evil is always present, and when you think about it, where else would the war claim the most casualties but on the front line— within the army of those most committed to goodness, truth, and light?

We mustn't excuse the wrongdoing or underplay its seriousness, but did we really think that all Christians were going to be squeaky clean and victorious all the time? Wouldn't you be suspicious if the history of the Church were 100 percent perfect? If it were, then it couldn't be real.

Seeing What Can Be

We need to be honest about the reality of good people doing bad things. Look in the mirror. Do you always live up to your highest ideals? Of course not. We all fail sometimes. Furthermore, whenever we pick out the bad things Christians have done we have to be fair and also see the good things too. For every immoral priest today there are a hundred noble and self-sacrificial priests. For every nun who is a bully there are a hundred who give their lives to serve the poor. For every corrupt pope in history there have been thousands of hard working, self-sacrificial, and holy popes.

The Church's holiness is real, even though it is soiled by sin. The Church is holy because it is on a holy mission. It is fighting the good fight, and is filled with the Holy Spirit to enable that fight to go on.

A mature person is neither a total pessimist nor a naive optimist, but rather looks at the whole picture. You see how things really are, but also how things *can be*. You see the real faults in yourself, in others, and in the world, but you also see the great potential in yourself, in others, and in the world.

The Church is holy in this sense because it helps us see both what we are and what we can be. The Church doesn't whitewash the human condition. It says boldly, "We are all sinners. We are lost in the dark and need someone to rescue us." But the Church also says, "We are all sons and daughters of the living God. We were created to be no less than the radiant inhabitants of heaven. Let us be all that we can be in the power of God, leaving behind the works of darkness and moving forward together into the full and abundant life that he has promised."

Chapter Four
Catholic Church

The Universal Corner Shop

If you want to discover the reality of the Catholic Church, you don't have to travel to Rome – that's simply where the international headquarters are located. Instead, discover your neighborhood Catholic parish church. There in your own town the one universal community of Christ's disciples has its local branch.

Your local Catholic parish is where the ancient, universal Church that Christ founded becomes real. There you will meet people who are struggling to fight the battle against evil and follow Christ. Just as marriage makes love real, so joining the Catholic Church makes real your commitment to Christ. When something is real it is both difficult and glorious. So it is with marriage and with being a Catholic. It is tough. It is a challenge. But then, did you expect the Christian life to be easy?

233

Here, There, and Everywhere

One good definition of the word "Catholic" is "universal." In other words, the Catholic Church is everywhere. It is not tied down to one particular region, country, or ethnic group. Over the centuries, by the power of the Holy Spirit, the Catholic community has permeated every continent. People have become Catholics from virtually every tribe, nationality, and race on earth.

As a result, there is a huge variety within the Catholic Church. If you go to South America or Africa you will find poor Catholics living in simple communities. They might worship in a church that is no more than a shed. Their music will be simple ethnic music and their prayers will be the prayers of the poor.

On the other hand, if you visit an affluent suburb in the United States or Europe you will find relatively wealthy Catholics in comfortable, modern churches or exquisite ancient cathedrals. Their struggle is to follow Christ despite having so much material wealth. Their challenge is to make generous sacrifices of both prayer and money to help their poor brothers and sisters on the other side of the world.

Contrasts like these can be multiplied over and over again. East and west, north and south, rich and poor, educated and uneducated, black and white, men and women, old people and children—in the Catholic Church they all exist together as the family of God.

Believing in a universal Church does not simply mean believing with our heads that such a worldwide family exists; it also means that we believe with our hearts that *we belong* to that family. It means that we become a living part of the vast and complex community of followers of Jesus Christ around the world and down the ages.

Salvation outside the Church?

It is a wonderful thing to belong to a family of people who are united in one faith, following one Lord and belonging to one church. But being a Catholic also means that we are members of the Body of Christ. As such we have a new power in our lives. We share in the same power that raised Jesus from the dead. Because we share in this power we are delivered from eternal death, and have the promise of eternal life with God.

Is that unfair to all those who are not Catholics? In the section on "one Church" I explained that all non-Catholic Christians who have faith in Christ, and who have been baptized into his death and resurrection, can also share in the hope of salvation. But there are many people who follow religions other than Christianity. Are they able to be saved or are they already damned?

There is also the question of all those who have never heard about Jesus Christ. Will God send them all to hell simply because they have never had the chance to have faith in Christ and be baptized? If so, it sounds very unfair.

Denial and Affirmation

Catholics recognize the goodness and truth in other religions. We recognize that the Jews, for example, are our older brothers and sisters in the faith. Jesus was a Jew. Christianity grew out of the Jewish religion. Catholics believe that a Jewish person's faith would be fulfilled and completed if he were to become a Christian, but we also recognize that God can draw faithful Jews to himself if it is his will. If he does so it is through Jesus Christ's victory over death.

Catholics also recognize that Muslims seek to follow the same God as Christians and Jews. Muslims follow the teachings of Mohammed as written in the Koran. We don't agree with everything they teach, and they certainly don't agree with everything that Catholics believe.

Catholics believe in goodness, truth, and beauty wherever it is found. Thus we realize that all other religions aren't 100 percent wrong. Instead we believe that the other world religions are good as far as they go, but that they are only ever a preparation for the fullness for God's truth as shown in Jesus Christ. In the other religions the truth is understood in a partial way. In Jesus Christ the truth has come in all its fullness.

Catholics are able to affirm these good things in other religions without denying the truths they hold to as Catholics. We are able to fight beside them in the battle against evil while at the same times helping them to fight it more effectively by sharing with them the full truth about what Jesus has done for us.

As for salvation, we know that God sent Jesus not to condemn the world, but to save the world. We pray that through Jesus' death and resurrection all people might be saved. Then we work hard to proclaim the good news of Jesus Christ to all people and we trust God to answer this prayer in his own way.

Us and Them

Christianity remains the largest world religion, but there are many other religions besides the Muslims and Jews. One can see how a Muslim or a Jew, who claims to worship the same God as Christians, might be closer to Christianity than people of other faiths.

You might wonder what happens to Buddhists, Sikhs, Bahai's, Hindus, pagans, animists, etc. They don't profess to worship the same God as the Christians. In the gospel Jesus says clearly that he is the only way to God the Father. If those who follow other religions do not believe in Jesus can they be saved?

A Universal Mission

The Catholic Church is the Universal Church, and that means that it has a universal mission. Before he went back to heaven Jesus commanded his followers to go into the whole world to proclaim the good news. He wanted everyone to be set free from their selfishness to attain a new and abundant life.

Catholics want to learn from non-Christian religions. We want to claim what is good in them and endorse all that is true and beautiful in their teachings. However, we are also aware that the Catholic system is the only one that is truly universal. In other words, all that is good, beautiful, and true within all the other religions can also be found within the Catholic faith.

If you knew someone who was digging a trench with a teaspoon you might applaud his efforts. You could acknowledge that he was doing an excellent job as far as his skill and his tools could allow. But if you had a spade or a bulldozer you would want to tell him about the even better tools that you had available, so that he could dig a better ditch in a fraction of the time.

This is how Catholics feel about Jesus' command to tell others the good news. For those who have never heard the news, the commandment is simple: tell everyone that God loves them and Jesus has come to set them free from selfishness and final death.

It *is* possible for a person of non-Christian faith to find salvation; but it will be the salvation won for them by Jesus Christ, whether they realize it or not. And that salvation is so much simpler and more rewarding to pursue by its right name. For those who follow other religions the process is like telling the person who is using a teaspoon to dig a ditch that there is a better, fuller way to complete the task.

Redeeming the Whole World

This is why the Catholic Church will always be a missionary church. Every Catholic—whether an ordinary

238

person or a priest, bishop, monk, or nun—is called to tell others the good news about Jesus Christ.

Our mission is to do nothing less than transform the world through the salvation of souls. Jesus died and rose again to set loose the power to effect that transformation. We, as his Body on earth today, are required to carry on his work and complete the job he gave us to do.

Each of us must get on with the job in the way best suited to our own personalities, gifts, and abilities. Some will help to redeem the world by telling people about Jesus Christ and helping them to have faith and come to be baptized.

Others will be busy transforming the world through political activity, or through education, health care, or social work. Others transform the world by bringing up many children who are on fire with the love of God. Still others will work to transform the whole world by giving their lives to prayer and worship.

No matter what our particular task, each one of us is called to transform the world by first of all being transformed ourselves. Do you want others to know the joy, power, and confidence that comes from having faith in Christ? Then show them the proof in your own transformed life.

The command to go out into the world and transform it by his power was the last word Jesus gave to his apostles. They bore his word and his power into the world; and we take part in the same mission because we share in the same faith that has been given to us by those very same apostles 2,000 years ago.

Chapter Five
Apostolic Church

A Firm Foundation

Jesus told a story about two men who built houses.
The first man found a cheap piece of sandy ground
and put up a nice house quite easily. The second man
invested in a rocky piece of high ground. It was hard
work to build the house in such a place, but the foundation was firm and sure. When the floods and rains came,
the man who built on sand saw his house fall down
while the man who built on rock was safe and secure.

Later in the New Testament, Paul says that the
Church is built on the foundation of the prophets and
apostles. What he means is that is that the community
of Christians is like the second man's house. It is built
carefully and with much hard work on a solid and
sure foundation. As Christians, our belief, our worship, and our work is rooted in the life and ministry
of Jesus' first followers.

Jesus had many followers and disciples, but from them he chose twelve for a special ministry of leadership. These twelve are called "apostles," which means "ambassadors" or "sent ones." Jesus gave the apostles authority to continue his work. He said that he was sending them just as God had sent him. He also promised to be with them forever, and to send the Holy Spirit to guide and strengthen them.

Therefore, when Jesus ascended into heaven, he left behind a group of men who would be his agents. As he was the hand of God, they would be his hands, his feet, his voice on earth. In the gospels we find that the apostles were given power to do what Jesus did in three ways. They were given the power to teach the truth faithfully. They were given power over the forces of evil, illness, and death. They were also given the power to forgive sins in Jesus' name.

The Successors of the Apostles

The New Testament book, *The Acts of the Apostles* tells us how these "sent ones" got on with the job. The story opens with the Day of Pentecost. The apostles were gathered with the other followers of Jesus wondering what would happen next. Suddenly the Holy Spirit came upon them in a glorious rush, and they received power for the task that Jesus had given them.

The apostle Peter emerged as their natural leader. He preached to crowds of people about Jesus and thousands responded to the good news, believed in

Jesus and were baptized. Eventually a prominent Jew named Paul was converted and joined the apostles. He was the first apostle of the next generation. Through a powerful conversion experience he also claimed to have been chosen by Christ and his calling was confirmed by the other apostles. Together, Peter and Paul helped to establish the Church. The other apostles went into the whole known world spreading the good news and starting local churches wherever they went.

Before long, throughout the Roman Empire, little groups of Christians were meeting in homes and local halls. The new little religion prospered and grew. Churches flourished and soon in the major cities there were many little cells of believers in Jesus Christ. The apostles appointed leaders in each city and it was natural for the leader the apostles appointed to become the leader of all the Christians in that city and surrounding area.

Jesus had promised to be with his followers forever, and the first generation of Christians realized that, after the death of the apostles, the power Jesus had given them had been passed on to the local church leaders they had appointed. The idea that leadership could be "handed on" from one leader to the next generation was a normal part of the culture of the day. As a result the leaders of the local churches (called bishops) were seen to be the natural successors of the apostles.

Built on the Rock

Paul said that the Church was built on the solid foundation of the prophets and apostles. He must have been thinking of a conversation Jesus had had with Peter. Peter's given name was Simon. But when he recognized that Jesus was the Son of God, Jesus responded by praising him and giving him a new name. From then on he was to be called "Peter" which means "Rock." Then Jesus said, "On this rock I will build my Church."

After he rose from the dead Jesus appointed Peter to the leadership role in a different way. He asked Peter three times to "feed my sheep." Jesus had already said that he was the Good Shepherd, and just before he went back to heaven he delegated to Peter his job as head Shepherd on earth.

Peter emerged as the natural leader after Jesus' return to heaven. Eventually he went to Rome and with Paul, helped establish the Church in the empire's capital city. The leaders of the Roman church were therefore seen to be the successors of Peter. Because he was the leader of the twelve apostles it was natural that his successors—the leaders of the Roman church—were also seen to be the leaders of the whole Church.

Catholics believe that there is still a successor of Peter active in the world today. The present-day Bishop of Rome is the Pope. The word Pope simply means "Papa." The Pope is our spiritual father on earth. He speaks today with the same voice of authority that Jesus gave to Peter 2,000 years ago.

Reliable Leadership

It is impossible for any organization to prosper without proper leadership. It is impossible for any army to win a war without a supreme commander. Likewise, the Church cannot have unity if it is not united under one leader. Jesus the Good Shepherd said that there would be, "one flock and one shepherd." He asked Peter to be that shepherd. We believe Peter's successor still plays the same unifying leadership role today.

The Pope is not an all-powerful, absolute monarch. The New Testament shows that Peter ruled by consulting the other apostles and deciding on matters together with them. Likewise, the Pope rules the Church through consultation with all the bishops of the world as well as through their consultation with all the priests and people. Yet it is not a democracy. It is a collaborative and consultative council with a leader at the top and a clear chain of command.

Jesus promised his followers that the Holy Spirit, the "Spirit of Truth," would come to them. In this way Jesus guaranteed to his followers a measure of his own ability to teach the truth without error. This same gift resides in the Church today. The bishops of the Church maintain, defend, develop, and teach the same truth that has been handed down to them from the apostles. Because of this historic truth we can rely on the Church to teach the truth about Jesus without error.

Written Answers

As I said earlier, the teaching of the Catholic Church is rooted in the faith, life, and ministry of the apostles. They were empowered and granted authority by Jesus himself. We believe that the Church today teaches with the same authority and is empowered by the same Holy Spirit.

One of the fruits of the Church's power to understand and teach the truth is the Bible. The Bible is a collection of Jewish and Christian religious writings. The Christians of the first few centuries gathered the stories of Jesus, and the letters that the apostles had written to the churches. They gathered the history of the apostles' lives and some other writings. Eventually they recognized that the Holy Spirit had helped the human authors write these unique witnesses to Jesus Christ.

These writings were granted special Church approval as the Sacred Scriptures or the Bible. The Bible then became a unique source book for further teachings. The leaders of the Church realized that the words of the Bible put them in intimate contact with the teachings of the apostles, and therefore with Jesus himself. The Scriptures gave them a firm guideline and measuring rod for the truth. Nothing they would preach or teach could ever contradict the meaning of what was taught in the Bible. If it did, they were wrong and not the Bible.

In addition to the written teaching of the apostles there was an unwritten body of teaching. The preachers and teachers of one generation handed down the teachings of the apostles in oral form. The Catholic Church maintains the apostolic tradition as another branch of authoritative apostolic teaching alongside the Bible.

The fullness of the Christian faith is expressed in the historic, full-blooded beliefs of the Catholic Church. These beliefs have been fully presented most recently in a book called the *Catechism of the Catholic Church*. This is a scholarly but readable and inspiring text that draws together the truths of the Bible and the truths of Christian tradition to express clearly what Catholics believe.

The *Catechism* is a clear collection of Catholic beliefs, but Catholic beliefs are not just "book knowledge." The Bible and the oral tradition of the Church are rooted in the living experience of the people of God. The Bible and tradition complement each other, and come alive as the Bible is read within the daily and weekly worship of the Church. It is good to read the Bible on our own, but we must always be aware that the Bible on its own can be interpreted in many different ways. Like statistics, it can mean almost anything to anybody. That is why Catholics always read the Bible in the context of the ongoing traditions of the Church. In that way, the Church that gave us the Bible also helps us to understand the Bible correctly.

Authority without Authoritarianism

We saw earlier that there are some 20,000 non-Catholic Christian denominations in the U.S. The reason there are so many different groups is because the leaders of these groups have all disagreed amongst themselves.

They disagree because they have looked only to the Bible for their source book, and they have read the Bible outside the context of the Church. The Bible alone does not have the authority to teach us without error. If it did, then there would not be 20,000 different non-Catholic denominations—each one of which claims to be really following the Bible!

When we say that the Catholic faith is "apostolic" we mean that we follow the faith of the apostles as expressed in the Bible, but we also believe that the Holy Spirit who inspired those apostles is still alive today. That same Spirit works through the teaching ministry of the Church. The Pope and the bishops of the Church are the successors of the apostles, and they are empowered to teach us how to understand the Christian faith in all its fullness. And we further believe that the pope has been given the special grace of *infallibility*.

When we say the pope is "infallible" we simply mean that when it comes to teaching matters of faith and morals, the pope has been given the gift to teach us God's truths without error. This doesn't mean the pope is a sinless person or that he never makes mistakes in ordinary areas of human opinion. It doesn't mean that he is all-knowing or that he channels God's words through his mouth. It simply means that when he does teach Catholic faith and morals, what he teaches will be reliable and true. In this way the integrity of Christ's teachings are assured of being faithfully preserved over time.

Dwight Longenecker

Chapter Six

Privileges and Duties

Where there's a Will There's a Way

Because the Church is One, Holy, Catholic, and
Apostolic we, as individuals have a duty to be One,
Holy, Catholic, and Apostolic.

These four descriptions of the Church help us to
understand our goal and destiny as Christians. I am
called as an individual to follow the faith that was
first taught by the apostles and has been handed
down to me through the ages.

The apostolic faith is found in the Bible, but it is
also available to me through the continued teaching
and preaching of the Church. When you go to Mass
the priest gives a homily that helps you to understand
how the apostolic faith applies to your life today.

Bishops regularly issue pastoral letters that help
maintain, defend, and apply the apostolic faith. The
pope writes and publishes encyclical letters that also

address particular concerns and help to apply the apostolic faith in the world today.

Finally, there is a wealth of Catholic material that helps to teach the apostolic faith. Books, television stations, videos, pamphlets, music, and websites all keep the apostolic faith alive and help you understand it and apply it better.

For Better or For Worse

The apostolic faith includes not only the religious truths about Jesus Christ and the Church, but also the teaching on how Christians should live.

Catholics have been blamed in the past for focussing too much on sin and making people feel guilty for what they've done wrong. It is true that some Catholic leaders have done this in an aggressive, even sour way. However, it is part of the Church's duty to show us where we're going wrong just as it is a doctor's duty to diagnose a serious illness correctly.

The doctor diagnoses cancer not because he wants you to die, but because he wants you to live. It is the same when the Church points out where our lives are going wrong. Church teachers and ministers have the courage to tell us what is wrong not because they want us to feel bad, but because they want us to get better.

Being a Christian means that we are constantly aware of our failings, but it also means we are constantly aware of God's help in our lives. Christians are keenly alert to their failures because they are so keenly alert to how much better life can be.

A Wider Vision

If we are called to follow the apostolic faith as individuals, we are also called to practice a *universal* faith. Being a Christian is not just about me and God or even about me and God and my local community. It is about me and God and the whole universe.

Being Catholic puts my own little life in perspective. My personality, my race, and my nationality are all part of a much wider family that includes every other background in the world. As such, I am responsible for these other Christians, and they are responsible for me. To be Catholic means that I must get involved in the lives of others.

In my personal life this means that I must respect others people. In the area of sexuality, no man or woman can be regarded as merely my sex toy. Neither can I exploit or use people by cheating them, stealing from them, or abusing them in any way. From now on every person is my brother or my sister.

This worldwide vision of my place in relationship with the whole of humanity affects other aspects of my life too. I must care for the poor, the disabled, the refugees, political prisoners, and the oppressed. God may call me to give my life serving these poor and outcast brothers and sisters of mine, or he may simply enable me to support others who work to help those who are less well off.

I cannot be complacent. My life is no longer my own. It has been given to me in order to help my brothers and sisters in this universal family of God called the Catholic Church.

Be Perfect as Your Father in Heaven is Perfect

Jesus told his apostles that they should be perfect as God is perfect. Talk about setting high standards! What he meant by this is that those of us who are members of the One, Holy, Catholic, and Apostolic Church are called not only to follow the apostolic faith, and not only to have a universal outlook, but to strive after real holiness.

Every day of our life should now have a new goal: we are taking a further step towards that wholeness or holiness that God has designed us to attain. This means that every word, action, thought, and decision must be focused to this aim.

This activity is empowered by the Holy Spirit, and the Holy Spirit's power is delivered to us through the ministry of the Church. Once we see that this is the goal, then all the other do's and don'ts of religion take their proper place. All the guidelines and commandments that the Church gives us are suddenly seen, not as ends in themselves, but as means to an end. Likewise, the sacraments of the Church cease to be religious duties and become events in which we receive the power to live the Christian life, and are transformed from within.

If we are called to be wholly holy, then the rules and disciplines of the religious life become as joyful and difficult for us as an athlete's training program. An athlete doesn't mind getting up early, keeping to a strict diet, and a grueling regime of exercise, because he has his eyes set on the goal. He knows what he wants to achieve, and the training is merely the tool to get there.

It is the same in the religious life. To be holy requires discipline in prayer, self sacrifice and study. It requires a constant check on our selfish instincts. This religious regime can become legalistic and dull, but it is meant to be as liberating and life-giving as the training of an athlete or mountain climber. Remember, running a race is exhilarating as well as exhausting; and an climbing a mountain may be dangerous, but it is also exciting.

That They May Be One

In his last hours Jesus prayed that his followers, "might be one as you and I Father, are one." In other words, Jesus wanted them to be united with him, but he also wanted them to be united with each other, and united within themselves.

We follow the apostolic faith, we maintain a universal outlook, we strive and train for holiness because we are seeking this essential unity of being. We want to be one within ourselves. We want to be one with each other. We want to be one with the whole of creation. We want to be one with God.

Dwight Longenecker

We begin to share in this unity through our worship in the Catholic Church. We make a commitment to attend Mass every week because that is where we get re-focused. At Mass the unity we long for actually exists—even if it is still imperfect. At Mass we join ourselves with Christ, we join ourselves with our Christian brothers and sisters and we join ourselves with God. "Communion" means "union with" or "union across," and so at Mass or Holy Communion, that union which will one day have an eternal dimension is made immediately real to us.

Transformation Starts at Home

Staying in touch with Christ, and then spreading his life and love throughout the world, leads to a final goal. We are called to a higher and greater destiny than any of us can imagine. We are destined to become the very sons and daughters of God. Each one of us, with all our sadness, failures, and regrets, is called to total redemption and transformation. Jesus Christ wants us to be made into his likeness and to share the radiance of his glory.

The beautiful thing about the Christian faith is that this glory is not found in the things that appear high and mighty. The glory is found instead in the things that are lowly and humble. The fact that God's son came to be born in a drafty stable says it all. The glory of heaven is always expressed in the simplicity of ordinary life.

256

CATHOLICISM / *Pure and Simple*

Therefore if we want to be transformed into the radiant glory of Christ we don't begin by striving for high and holy religious experiences. We don't attempt great feats of prayer, abstinence, and self-denial. We don't lock ourselves away pursuing a purified spiritual existence. Instead we get on with ordinary life—but now in an extraordinary way.

Christ's glory shining out of the ordinary life of a carpenter in Nazareth 2,000 years ago reminds us that it is in our ordinary tasks, trials, and tribulations that our transformation will take place. So be ordinary in an extraordinary way. Connect with Christ in the ordinary, sometimes fascinating and sometimes tiresome duty of attending Mass every week. Living this extraordinarily ordinary life means we see the chance to be like Christ by getting up early to make breakfast, helping others even when they didn't ask, and living a life of simple self sacrifice every day.

It is by being ourselves that we are transformed beyond ourselves. It is by following Christ in our everyday lives that we become like him, and it is through a lifetime of this simple spiritual life that we are able to transform the whole world.

Chapter Seven
Further Up and Further In

The Long and Winding Road

The spiritual way is not the easiest path through life. Jesus said the way was narrow and there are few who find it. On the other hand, he said the way to spiritual destruction was a broad downward slope. It is easy to slide into hell. It is difficult to climb into heaven.

Is anything good ever easy? What great thing has ever been done overnight? It is true that we are called to a glory beyond our imagining. It is true that we are called to be radiant and everlasting beings—no less than sons and daughters of God himself, but it is also true that we have a long way to go.

When you think about it, is there really anything else worth living for? Physical pleasure fades. Money is only good in this life. Status and fame disappear. Even our dearest human loves will be snatched away by illness and death. Our only hope is to be united with all that we love in a greater reality beyond the grave. The spiritual life therefore not only leads to a happier existence here, but it offers the only hope for a happier existence on the other side of death.

That happy existence is not guaranteed simply because we happen to want it. Jesus Christ has opened up the way to eternal life. He has given it to us as a gift, but that treasure must be sought and found. The treasure is free, but we must study the map and go on the long journey to find it. Living our lives for this end is the best investment anyone can ever make.

Moving Into God's Glory

The exciting truth about following the spiritual path is that every day we are making further progress towards all that we have ever loved and longed for in life. Every path leads somewhere, and if we are following the way of Christ, then he is not only the way; he is also the destination.

Heaven is not simply a happy place on the other side of the clouds where we will see all our loved ones again. Heaven is the fulfillment of all our hopes and dreams. It is a reality that makes everything on this earth seem like a dream.

Some people say you make your own heaven and hell here on earth. This is true in one sense, but it is more true to say that you are choosing between heaven or hell every day here on earth. You are choosing heaven or hell because every day—indeed every moment—you are choosing whether you wish to live God's way or your way. If you wish to live God's way, then that way will logically lead to God. If you choose to live your way, then your choice naturally leads away from God.

To choose heaven therefore, is not a "once and done" choice. It is a "once and done over and over again" choice. Will we choose to connect with Jesus at Mass and confession, or will we ignore him? Will we choose to give our money and time to a just cause or will we spend our resources solely for our own pleasure? Will we give of ourselves for the good of others or simply pursue our own desires? Every day will we choose to live our lives with, in and through the life of Christ, or will we go it alone? Down one route lies heaven. Down the other, hell.

The Slippery Slope

Is there such a place as hell? Will people really be tormented forever with pain and fire? It is not pleasant to think about hell, but when you do think about it, it becomes clear that hell is a necessity. If heaven is a place of goodness and justice, then there must be a place for all those who, all their lives, have run from all that is good, true and just.

Does God send people to hell? It is more likely that he simply gives each of us what we always wanted. If some people flee from goodness, truth, beauty and love all their lives can we imagine that they would *want* to go to heaven? If they have run away from God their whole life, then when they met him face to face they would surely flee from the intensity of his presence, and if they run from his presence, the only place to run would be the place where he is not present, and that place would be hell.

Perhaps then it is simply the case that the light of God is the same light to those who are saved and those who are damned. The only difference is that for those who have always loved goodness, truth, and beauty the light will be the light of Christ, while for those who have always loved evil, the same light will be experienced as the searing flames of hell.

Whatever hell consists of, we can say that it must be the everlasting torture of being left alone without God, without love, without beauty, without goodness and without truth. If we have choice, then we must have the choice to go there. If we do any action that, by its very nature, takes us away from God, and if we persist in that action without ever acknowledging that we are wrong, we are in danger of ending up with the fruit of that action—and that fruit is a future cut off from God, from life and from love.

The Third Way

Talking about heaven and hell in such black and white terms makes people uncomfortable. In one sense there is nothing wrong with that. Hell is meant to be uncomfortable, and the best sermon ever preached about hell consists of only two words: "Fear hell."

However, people are also uncomfortable because we realize that things are not so black and white. Each one of us might long for heaven, but we also stumble and fall into our darker desires, laziness, and selfishness. The condition of our hearts is not so clear-cut. If we are honest we admit that we are not saintly enough to go straight to heaven, but we also hope that we are not wicked enough to head for hell. To see ourselves this way is not proud or unduly humble. It is realistic.

This is why the Church teaches that there is a place called purgatory. "Purgatory" simply means a place of purgation or cleansing. Everybody in purgatory will eventually make it to heaven. It's just that they need some time to get their act together. If you like, purgatory is a place to wash up before mealtime. It is a place where our failures, imperfections, and faults can continue to be put right by the help of God's gift of grace. As long as we have sought God's way in this life; as long as we have put our trust in Christ's saving work, we can have a confident hope that after a time being cleaned up we will enter into the final glory of God's presence.

All Shall be Well

This final hope is the glory and joy of all Christians. We do not simply wish for pie in the sky and a happy hunting ground after we pass on. Instead heaven is the fulfillment of everything good on earth. There, all that is divided shall be one. There, all that was soiled and impure shall be holy and wholly itself. There, all that was small and narrow-minded will be universal in it scope and vision.

The vision of heaven in the New Testament has the apostles and prophets on thrones around the throne of God. This is a symbolic way of saying that heaven will be a fulfillment of all that the Church hints at here on earth. The welcome home we receive when we become Catholics is just a hint of the greater welcome home we shall receive on entry into heaven.

Heaven will be like a great family reunion, or a vast wedding reception. Everyone will be gathered in the unity for which they were created. At that point the transformation of every soul will be complete. Each one of us will be fully and wholly ourselves because we have found our rightful place in the great plan of God for all things.

Then we shall see clearly. All will be reconciled. We will see that all is well. We will understand that even the sins and sorrows and terrors were part of the greater plan. Then all shall be joy and a powerful peace, for the battle will be done, the long journey ended. We shall be home at last, and the celebration to welcome the long lost child will begin.

ADDITIONAL READING

If you enjoyed *Catholicism: Pure & Simple* why not check out Fr. Longenecker's other books? You can order any of them through his website: **www.dwightlongenecker.com**

The Path to Rome Fr. Longenecker used to be an Anglican priest. After he converted to the Catholic faith in 1995 he edited this collection of conversion stories.

Sixteen people tell how and why they became Catholics. From a former Anglican Bishop of London, to a woman Salvation Army Officer, from EWTN host Marcus Grodi to an Anglican priest's wife they all tell their moving and inspiring stories of why they took The Path to Rome

More Christianity Evangelical Christians love the Lord Jesus Christ and follow him with honest and open hearts. However, there is more to the Christian faith. Catholics affirm all the good things Evangelicals affirm, they just don't deny some of the things Evangelicals deny.

Fr. Longenecker was brought up as an Evangelical and attended Bob Jones University. He understands Evangelicals and in this book he explains the Catholic faith to Evangelicals with good humor, grace, simplicity and clarity. He's not concerned to prove Evangelicals wrong. Instead he urges them to move from 'Mere Christianity' to something more.

**New Edition
Coming Soon!**

Mary—A Catholic/Evangelical Debate
Twenty years after graduating from Bob
Jones University Dwight Longenecker met
up with an old college buddy through the
internet. By this time Dwight was a Catholic
and David Gustafson was an Evangelical
attending an Episcopal Church. After many
months debating religion by email, Dwight
and David decided to put their minds to
writing a book on the Blessed Virgin Mary.

David takes the Protestant side of the
debate and Dwight explains and defends all
the Catholic beliefs and practices regarding
the Virgin Mary. With introductions from
Protestant scholar J.I.Packer and Catholic Fr.
Richard John Neuhaus, this book is a readable but well researched study of everything
you always wanted to know about Mary.

*St. Benedict and St. Therese—The Little
Rule and the Little Way* During his time
living in England, Fr. Longenecker developed a great interest in both St. Benedict
and St. Therese of Lisieux. This book
studies the lives and writings of these two
beloved saints.

St. Benedict is like the grandfather in the
family of God and Therese is like his little
grandchild. Together they complement one
another and show us how to find God in the
ordinary things of life.

Listen My Son—St. Benedict for Fathers
As a father of four children and a Benedictine oblate, Fr. Dwight Longenecker is ideally suited to apply the famous *Rule of St. Benedict* to family life.

This book of daily readings give the reader a portion from the *Rule of St. Benedict* for each day. After the portion from the Rule there is a short reading that applies the timeless wisdom of St. Benedict to modern family life. This is a great gift for fathers of all ages.

Adventures in Orthodoxy This unusual book take the reader on a Chestertonian rollercoaster ride through the Apostle's Creed. Fr Longenecker goes on a creative quest for truth showing that orthodox Christianity is anything but dull. Instead it is a wide open, exciting explanation for all that was, all that is, and all that shall be.

Noted biographer Joseph Pearce has said, "In this exciting book Longenecker follows in the imaginative footsteps of Chesterton and Lewis. He sees and seizes the thrill of truth with insights of pyrotechnic brilliance. He shows us that orthodoxy is dynamic and thrilling. Hold on tight and enjoy the ride!"

Praying the Rosary for Inner Healing
God has used this book to touch thousands
of lives. In a very practical and simple way,
Fr Longenecker shows how the twenty
mysteries of the rosary connect with the
different stages of our lives. Step by step, this
book helps the reader meditate on the stages
of Christ's life and open their deepest areas
of their lives to the healing graces of Christ.

With inspiring illustrations by Catholic
artist Chris Pelicano, *Praying the Rosary for
Inner Healing* has been featured on the Spirit
Daily website and on Johnette Benkovic's
Living His Life Abundantly. It gives new
direction for those already used to praying
the rosary and shows newcomers how to use
this ancient and beautiful form of prayer in a
relevant and life changing way.

A Sudden Certainty—Priest Poems This
is a collection of Fr. Longenecker's poems.
Written in traditional forms, but with a con-
temporary voice, Fr. Longenecker meditates
on spiritual images alive in the ordinary life
of a priest.

Each poem is a little window into a new
way of seeing reality. Each page shows the
reader a fresh way of connecting with God's
light and love alive in the ordinary world.

In addition to his books, Fr. Longenecker writes regularly for *The National Catholic Register, This Rock Magazine, St Austin Review, Inside Catholic* and other websites. His popular and award winning blog, *Standing on My Head* is based on G.K.Chesterton's idea that, "Any scene can be more freshly and clearly seen when it is seen upside down."

Fr. Dwight has appeared on EWTN, Catholic radio and on broadcasts in England and across the USA. He speaks regularly and conferences and leads retreats on a variety of topics. Many audiences like to hear how he went from Bob Jones University to being a Catholic priest. Others ask him to lead retreats on the Benedictine and Theresian spirituality. He is also asked to lead workshops and seminars on apologetics, praying the rosary for inner healing, and his film-based seminars on *How to Be a Spiritual Hero*.

Fr. Longenecker's latest book, *The Quest for the Creed* is published by Crossroads in Autumn 2012. This new edition of his book *Adventures in Orthodoxy* will be followed by publication in Spring 2013 of the sequel, *The Romance of Religion*. He is working on a sequel to *The Gargoyle Code—Slubgrib Instructs*, trying to write his first novel, and is nurturing a screenplay on Shakespeare the Catholic.

Contact Fr. Longenecker through his website:
www.dwightlongenecker.com

BIOGRAPHICAL NOTE

Fr. Dwight Longenecker is an American who has spent most of his life living and working in England. After graduating from the fundamentalist Bob Jones University with a degree in Speech and English, he went to study theology at Oxford University. He was eventually ordained as an Anglican priest and served as a curate, a school chaplain in Cambridge and a country parson.

Realizing that he and the Anglican Church were on divergent paths, in 1995 Fr. Dwight and his family were received into the Catholic Church. He spent the next ten years working as a freelance Catholic writer, contributing to over twenty-five magazines, papers and journals in Britain, Ireland and the USA.

In 2006 Fr. Dwight accepted a post as Chaplain to St Joseph's Catholic School in Greenville, South Carolina. This brought him and his family back, not only to his hometown, but also to the American Bible belt, and hometown of Bob Jones University. In December of that year he was ordained as a Catholic priest under the special pastoral provision for married former Anglican clergy. He is now the parish priest of Our Lady of the Rosary Church in Greenville.

Fr. Dwight enjoys movies, blogging, books, and visiting Benedictine monasteries. He's married to Alison. They have four children—Benedict, Madeleine, Theodore and Elias. They live in Greenville, South Carolina with assorted pets including two labradors named Anna and Felicity.

Made in the USA
Lexington, KY
28 March 2015